Miracle *on* Cary Street

RESTORING VIRGINIA'S GRANDEST MOVIE PALACE

A MEMOIR

BY DUANE K. NELSON

Published by Little Star
Richmond, VA

Miracle on Cary Street: Restoring Virginia's Grandest Movie Palace is creative
nonfiction memoir. It reflects the author's current recollections of
experiences over time. Some names and characteristics have been changed,
some events have been compressed, and some dialogue has been created.
This is not an authorized account of the Byrd's restoration.

ISBN 978-1-7358872-0-3

Cover and interior design by Wendy Daniel.
Cover photo: Sky Noir photography by Bill Dickinson - www.skynoir.com

Printed in the United States of America

for Annemarie and Mark Couture, for whom without, there would be no Hope. You have always been there to help make all of my many dreams become realities.

Contents

Letter to the Whitten Family

September 17, 2014

Sara Jo and Jimmy Whitten
Whitten Brothers of Richmond
10701 Midlothian Tpke.
Richmond, VA 23235

Dear Sara Jo, Jimmy and the Whitten family,

I was very sad to hear of the passing of Miles. Unfortunately, I have visited Richmond only once since leaving in 2007. I was fortunate to be able to visit with Miles at that time. Until about three months ago, I was able to speak with him by phone quite often. I'd like to share a few thoughts with all of you.

I had the pleasure of first meeting Miles in 1981. He introduced me to the Byrd Theatre. His history with the Byrd started much earlier—probably sometime in the 1950s. As I remember his telling me, he studied Liberal Arts and Theatrical Staging at the College of William & Mary. After WWII, he moved to Richmond to help his father run the family business. Had he instead moved to New York to pursue theater, he probably would have become one of this country's most celebrated Broadway set designers. New York's loss was Richmond's, and the Byrd's, gain. What good fortune his presence turned out to be.

Miles's relationship with the Byrd started soon after he moved to Richmond. He became its caretaker and relief manager. And did the Byrd ever need a good caretaker! Even in the '50s the Byrd was at least a quarter of a century old and in constant need of repair. Miles did such a great job keeping the Byrd looking beautiful.

He was so well respected by Neighborhood Theatres Company,

operators of the Byrd, that he was given a lifetime pass to all of their movie presentations in any of their theatres. When I wanted a job with Neighborhood Theatres, Miles made a single phone call. Within an hour Morton Thalhimer, President, and Sam Bendheim, Vice president of Neighborhood Theatres, called me to ask me when I wanted to start. Miles told them an interview wasn't necessary.

Over the course of the next two years, Neighborhood Theatres taught me how to manage a movie theatre; Miles taught me how to entertain the theatregoers. In short: showmanship.

In 1983, Neighborhood Theatres closed the Byrd Theatre after 54 years of continuous operations. They had been carrying the Byrd financially for some time. They did not close the Byrd because of poor management, but more because of the trend to multi-screen, away from single screen theaters. So now, the Byrd was not only old and decrepit, she was an albatross and closed. She had no heat, which is bad for the plaster. She was in need of a lot of love, attention, care, and vision.

The Byrd Theatre seemed doomed, just waiting for the wrecking ball. However, there were several things going in the Byrd's favor. There was Jerry Cable, who had the financial resources and a passion for historic properties. There was Gary Cowardin who had the technical skills to maintain and operate all of the electrical and mechanical systems in the Byrd. There was David Barnett, with the marketing and advertising skills necessary to rebrand an old theatre no one wanted to patronize into a newly restored theatre that everyone wanted to patronize. And finally, there was Miles Rudisill. Miles knew the art of historic restoration, preservation, and theatrical showmanship. Miles introduced me to all of these men, except for Jerry Cable.

Where did the Byrd vision come from? It originally came from Miles.

I first met Miles before I became involved with the Byrd Theatre. He gave me a book, *The Best Remaining Seats*, written by his close friend, Ben Hall. *The Best Remaining Seats* illustrates the architecture of the few great remaining movie palaces and of many of the movie palaces razed in the 1950s and 1960s. The focus of the book was New York's famed Roxy Theatre. The Roxy was a movie palace and was the inspiration for the Byrd when the Byrd reopened her doors in April 1984.

The Byrd originally opened in 1928, two years later than the Roxy. The restoration vision of the Byrd Theatre in 1984 was to bring back the flair and the persona of the 1920s. All of the antiques purchased and incorporated in the Byrd were of that era. The concession counter came from a drug store established in the 1920s. Also from the 1920s were the lamps, chairs, and fixtures. All of the ushers wore period tuxedos and all of the concessionaires wore flapper outfits.

We even had our own chorus line. Instead of calling them the Roxyettes, later to be called the Rockets after the famed Radio City Music Hall, we called them the Byrdettes. The Byrdettes performed to packed houses in all of our Easter and Christmas shows until 1989. It was actually the 1989 Christmas Spectacular, performed under the musical direction of Doug Richards and the Great American Music Ensemble that garnered the attention of the Disney Co., which resulted in the use of Byrd exclusively to exhibit Disney films in the early 1990s. The Byrd Theatre started getting busy. Throughout the 1990s it averaged over 10,000 patrons a week.

The Byrd never looked better! Miles worked every day repairing seats, chipped plaster, torn fabric, worn out carpet, broken furniture, burned out bulbs and more. And the roof—we'd all be millionaires if we had a dollar for every bucket of water Miles emptied from the leaking roof. Better yet, we could have paid for a new roof.

There wasn't anything Miles couldn't fix, mend or replace, restoring it back to its original condition and look of the 1920s. He was obsessed with keeping the Byrd beautiful, saving it for the future. He was obsessed with providing Richmond with a movie palace, the showplace of Virginia. He was obsessed with taking patrons back in time, when movie palaces took everyone away from the rigors of life and offered hope for the future.

Miles was instrumental in two things that were absolutely necessary in saving the Byrd Theatre. First, he was able to place the Byrd on the "Register of Interiors for Historic Properties." He did that on his own in 1977. Second, he helped me form the Byrd Theatre Foundation in 2002. This took us every bit of two years to accomplish, but that we did. Now the Byrd has a means of raising the necessary resources to preserve her for the future.

Miles never received a dime for his countless hours of hard work; in a sense that made him a volunteer. But if it weren't for Miles, I know there would be no Byrd today. The Byrd Theatre will miss him; Richmond will miss him; those of us who knew him will miss him, not least of all me! Even if the foundation were to raise tens of millions of dollars to restore her, she will never look as beautiful as when Miles was there.

Sincerely,

Duane Kennedy Nelson

"My brother, Miles Rudisill, was the adoptive father of the Byrd Theater in Richmond, Virginia. He had no children, no wife, or other family commitments. The Byrd was his life and he cared for it as would his child.

Once there was a small tear in one of their huge heavy velvet curtains, and Miles asked me to repair it. It was quite a job to work on- that huge piece of velvet on my little home sewing machine. But anything for the Byrd!

How nice that a book has been written that honors his many years of dedication in preserving such a wonderful Richmond landmark."

– Sara Jo Whitten

PROLOGUE
Duane Kennedy Nelson

Every so often God chooses an individual, gives them a purpose, and gives them a mission to perform in life. Sometimes that person is the most unqualified and undeserving person in the world.

I feel that I was that individual chosen to perform the mission of saving the Byrd. I am grateful to have been the one chosen.

I managed the Byrd Theatre from 1982 to 1989 and then owned the management operation of the Byrd Theatre for close to eighteen years.

This is the story of the redevelopment, restoration and operation of the Byrd Theatre during my twenty-five-year tenure. It is also the story of the vision and means of making that vision possible for the continuous operation and salvation of the Byrd Theatre for many years and generations to come.

This story is true to the best of my knowledge and includes many names of the people who contributed so much to the Byrd Theatre.

CHAPTER ONE
New to Richmond

I remember when I first met her.

It was a miserable, wet, late October night in 1981. I had been working for Chris Oley at Shields Market across from Joe's Inn in the Fan for a couple of months.

I enjoyed the job. It didn't provide much responsibility, but it allowed me the opportunity to continue an education and be around some interesting people who lived in the Fan.

Miles Rudisill lived around the corner and came into the market on a daily basis. Rudisill was a retired history teacher who previously worked in the family wholesale florist business. He lived on Hanover Avenue and often invited me to visit him on his way home from work.

I lived on Park Avenue, near Virginia Commonwealth University. I usually walked to and from Shields Market by way of Grove Avenue. I was sweet on a girl along that path and it was several months before I took Rudisill up on his offer to take a different path along Hanover Avenue. But one day I did, and what an eye-opening experience it turned out to be.

Rudisill's house was decorated like a movie palace. I didn't know what a movie palace looked like back then; the closest thing to a movie palace I had ever seen was the Grandin Theatre in Roanoke, Virginia.

Most of the furniture's designs were Victorian, Antebellum, and Art Deco. There were Tiffany and Tiffany-style lamps; everything in red and gold lace (lots of gold lace), high ceiling draperies and plenty of candelabras and chandeliers. Rudisill even had a model of a movie palace stage, complete with a moving orchestra pit, musicians and a theatre pipe organ. This was in the library with a thousand books. Next to the library was a music room with a 1921 Weber reproducing grand piano.

I gathered that Rudisill didn't make his money as a school teacher.

One night I stayed late reading in his library. I'll never forget the book, because it was a book that changed my life.

The Last Remaining Seats by Ben Hall was about the many movie palaces razed during the 1960s and 1970s; it focused heavily on The Roxy Theatre in New York.

The Roxy was a splendid example of an American Movie Palace. The Roxy ranked right up there with such palaces as the Loews and Fox theatres.

It was after midnight when Rudisill asked, "Do you want to see a real movie palace, 'The Show Place of Virginia?'"

Of course I was all for it and in a matter of minutes, we were off.

We drove south a few blocks, turned right and traveled west on Main Street. We crossed the Boulevard, where Main Street turns into Ellwood Avenue, and then turned left on Sheppard Street. This brought us to Cary Street where we turned left and pulled up in front of the Byrd Theatre.

We were at the beginning of Carytown. Most of the street lamps were out; most of the shops were closed and boarded up. If I hadn't known better, I would have thought we were on an abandoned movie set on some forgotten backlot. Back then, Carytown looked (and felt) like a ghost town.

The Byrd was closed; the last show had been out for a while. We entered through the front doors to the right of the box office.

The doors were black and I had no idea they were plated brass underneath. During the Byrd's heyday, polishers worked around the clock to keep those brass doors shined and polished. But it was clear that those days were long gone.

Next up was the foyer and then the lobby. This may sound strange, but the first thought that came to my mind was the smell. There was a strange odor.

I figured it was a mix of mildew and mold, but there were other layers to the aroma. Maybe it was an odd blend of cola syrup and popcorn butter that saturated the carpets and walls.. Maybe it was the decades of decay from a leaking roof and dirty footprints from generations of patrons. But it was a smell of death; something you might catch a whiff of in a crypt; a smell that belonged in a Bram Stoker novel.

What also belonged in a crypt was the plywood concession counter that took up most of the lobby. What an eyesore!

I would find out later that the counter matched the other Neighborhood Theatres' concession counters of the 1960s in appearance and inefficiency.

Rudisill left me for a moment to turn the lights on. He flipped on all of the lights in the lobby, one large chandelier in the lobby, and two smaller chandeliers on the mezzanine. This almost knocked me off my feet. I noticed about a dozen wall sconces and beautiful hand-painted murals. There was marble and brass everywhere. Although much of the brass was unpolished, it didn't matter. The real beauty was yet to come.

Rudisill disappeared again up the right hand grand stairway. He was gone for five minutes and when he reappeared, he opened two sets of brass doors and we entered the auditorium.

Years later I would see *The Wizard of Oz* in full color at the Byrd, but going into the Byrd's auditorium for the first time, I felt like Dorothy opening the front door to Oz. It was stunning.

The first thing I saw after clearing the balcony overhang, was the magnificent main chandelier. It's eighteen feet tall and over twelve feet in diameter, adorned with some two thousand pieces of Czechoslovakian crystal and lamped with four circuits and hundreds of colored bulbs.

Looking up and around, I saw two large alcoves and six smaller ones lining the sixty foot high walls. Each of the smaller alcoves contained hand-painted murals and smaller chandeliers. The larger alcoves contained a grand piano and a harp, with hand-painted murals beneath large chandeliers. A large gold curtain hung below the proscenium arch. The entire interior was painted in a gold colored metal leaf.

The Byrd was well preserved, but she showed signs of wear and tear.

One of the first things I noticed was that large areas of seating were closed off to the public. Whenever and wherever the roof leaked, plaster fell. To keep patrons from getting injured, the theatre's staff simply roped off the affected areas.

When plaster gets wet, it falls in chunks. Sometimes those pieces are large enough to cause real harm, especially when falling from more than five stories overhead. Wet plaster was a huge problem at the Byrd and their inability to access the damaged areas prevented the owners from fixing the problem.

In the early 1970s, the owners of the Byrd felt that the roof needed to be addressed. Not that the roof leaked at the time, but after more than forty years of neglect, they figured it was time to do something.

What did they do? They put another roof on top of the old one.

This was a standard re-roofing practice of a flat roof for the time. But, unless done correctly and ventilated properly, the two roofs would expand and contract, creating cracks that would lead to a leaky roof.

Water destroys plaster like cancer destroys human tissue. So, from the early 1970s, after the placement of the second roof, the roof leaked. Little did I know, this would cause me many sleepless nights in the years to come.

Speaking of sleeplessness, I didn't do much snoozing that night. I lay awake with a head full of possibilities. Dreams of being the next "Roxy" intertwined in my mind with ambitions of fame and fortune.

CHAPTER TWO
Neighborhood Theatres

S everal weeks later, Rudisill talked with me about a career in the movie theatre management business.

Rudisill had influence with Neighborhood Theatres. He arranged an interview for me with President Morton Thalhimer and Vice President Sam Bendheim.

I really didn't know what to expect going into the interview. Neighborhood Theatres had been in business in Richmond, Virginia since the invention of silent movies back in the early 1900s. Both Thalhimer and Bendheim were household names and influential in the community. Their fathers started Neighborhood Theatres with only a handful of locations. The chain had grown to over a hundred theaters and was still growing.

I was barely 21, with an engineering degree and some work experience primarily in food service. I was hardly an ideal candidate for theatre management.

What I didn't realize at the time was that I already had the job. Rudisill had arranged it all. Years later I would find out how influential Rudisill was in "the business."

First on the agenda was going through a training program. The best man to train me for the job was Tom Connell, who had been a manager for Neighborhood Theatres for a long time.

Connell managed the Willow Lawn Theatre. The Willow Lawn Theatre was located between Monument Avenue and Broad Street at the western end of the city. It was a twin screen theatre that opened in 1956, was busy, and proved to be a wonderful training ground.

When I first arrived, the theatre was in its tail end run of a re-release of *The Empire Strikes Back*. The theatre's next movie showing was *Tootsie*. *Tootsie* did an incredible business.

I went through the training program at an accelerated rate. My stay under Connell's tutelage only lasted several months, but what I learned stayed with me for life.

As Connell often said, "We can teach you managerial accounting; that's easy. But, training a manager to work with the public is difficult and can't be taught."

Man, was he right!

My next position was "Relief Manager." My primary responsibility was to take over the management responsibilities of theatres whose managers were on a leave of absence. This could be for many reasons such as vacation, promotion, medical leave, or dismissal. Most of my relief work was done due to promotion and vacation.

During the early 1980s, most theatre chains were moving from single screen operations to multi-screen operations. This was a trend to improve the economics of movie theatre operations and reduce the risk in screening exhibition.

My last stop as a relief manager for Neighborhood Theatres was the Byrd Theatre.

Mark Lyvely, the Byrd's current manager had been promoted to be the assistant manager at the Ridge Cinema. This was a tremendous promotion for Lyvely; it meant more responsibility and more pay. As I mentioned, Neighborhood Theatres during the early eighties was moving out of single screen theatre operations towards multi-screen theatre operations. At this time, the Ridge Cinema was a four screen operation with three more screens being added.

A lot goes into closing down a theatre. The Byrd had a long history, a successful run, and was well liked in the central Richmond area. It was at one time the catalyst property for the Carytown shopping area and the movie entertainment attraction for the entire Fan and Windsor Farms residential areas of Richmond.

But by the early 1980s, Carytown and the Byrd were now dead.

What used to be a bustling area of town filled with shopping and dining was now boarded up and riddled with crime. What used to be a crowded theater for close to fifty years was now sparsely attended. And the area it was in was considered dangerous and undesirable.

When I first arrived at the Byrd in the summer of 1982, Neighborhood Theatres was operating the movie palace as a second run repertory house. Floyd Davis, Neighborhood's booking agent, was primarily bringing in classic films and showing them at a discounted rate, probably around a two dollar admission price.

Ray Bentley, well known in the area for his midnight movie promotions, printed flyers and distributed them around town as a means of advertising the upcoming fare.

Although it was a gallant effort, the results were less than mediocre. Some nights, the attendance was so small or nonexistent, I would close the movie theatre by 9:00 p.m. Quite often, there would be nobody in attendance on Mondays and Tuesdays.

Eddie Weaver played the theatre pipe organ nightly, sometimes to a theater full of empty seats. A common practice was to run the film with sound only to keep lamp lighting costs down. Since the theatre was a Union house, the projectionists were paid whether the theatre was open for business or not.

Neighborhood Theatres' main goal for the Byrd Theatre was to keep the financial losses to a minimum. The lease was up at the end of 1982 and by that time, Neighborhood Theatres would have their expanded operations placed at the Ridge Cinemas in the West End of Richmond, property that they owned, not leased.

There were so many reasons the move made sense: the West End was a more populated area, taxes there were lower, and there was plenty of room to expand.

Unfortunately, my responsibilities in 1982 were to close the Byrd Theatre: to transplant or retire the staff; to remove all of the inventories, advertising materials, etc.; and to make way for the new owners/operators of the theatre.

Fortunately, Neighborhood Theatres consisted of ethical and civic-minded business people, and so even though in accordance with the conditions of the lease, the Byrd Theatre didn't have to be vacated as an operational movie theatre, it was.

And also fortunately for the Byrd Theatre, there was hope and there was a beginning to an incredible vision not too far in the future.

CHAPTER THREE
Jerry Cable

In the summer of 1997, Jerry Cable opened the Tobacco Company Restaurant in the Shockoe Slip area of Richmond, Virginia.

The restaurant was a phenomenal success when it opened. Now, some forty years later, it's still a phenomenal success and one of the most visited restaurants and landmarks in Richmond.

The success of the Tobacco Company is thanks to Cable's ingenious approach of integrating the beauty of historic architecture with antiques positioned in an interior design that really works.

The Tobacco Company was no longer a warehouse designed to deliver tobacco goods. Cable reimagined it as a warehouse designed to deliver hospitality and entertainment in a casual/fine dining enriched experience.

The reason so many investors wanted to be a part of Jerry Cable's ideas and were willing to finance his many projects? His endeavors made money. So, when Cable visited the Byrd Theatre for the first time, he envisioned a supper club, a dinner theatre, a place for theatre, dance and music.

In addition to the Tobacco Company Restaurant, Cable also owned and operated many properties, including residential buildings, bakeries, and even a plantation that quarried millions of dollars in mineral rights a year.

Getting involved with Cable would be an incredible experience for an aspiring entrepreneur.

The ultimate course the Byrd Theatre would take would be altered many times over the eighteen months the theatre was closed.

Cable wanted the Byrd to be a dinner theater or a supper club, but there were problems with that concept. In Virginia, restaurants were required to prepare and serve hot food in order to sell the higher-profit-margin items associated with alcohol sales.

Simply put, you can't run an establishment that exclusively serves alcohol. The Byrd would need a kitchen. This could have been remedied by buying adjacent properties to the Byrd in order to build a kitchen … if there were any adjacent properties available.

A rule of thumb in the restaurant industry: for every square foot of dining space, one square foot of kitchen space is recommended. The French cuisine envisioned for the Byrd Theatre would certainly complement the French Empire interior, but there was no space in or around the Byrd for a decent-sized kitchen.

Also unfortunate? Serving food in a theatre setting would mean only one turn a night. For most high volume restaurants, like the Tobacco Company Restaurant, turning tables over two and a half times a night is necessary to see a profit.

If we wanted the Byrd Theatre revitalized, restored and generating revenue, Cable needed investors with deep pockets.

CHAPTER FOUR
Irma and Samuel Warren

Cable introduced me to Samuel and Irma Warren just before Neighborhood Theatres vacated the Byrd in 1982.

The Warrens were the new owners and appeared to have the deep pockets every entrepreneur dreams about. They were nicknamed 'The Hillbillies" after the popular television show, "The Beverly Hillbillies."

I was told that for generations they owned a farm where Washington Dulles International Airport now sits.

Not only did Cable influence the Warrens into buying the Byrd, but he convinced them to invest in other properties in the Richmond area and Tampa, Florida, as well. The property in Tampa would ultimately mold the future of the Byrd Theatre; and change the financial futures of many of those who were involved.

The Byrd closed her doors in December, 1982 having run almost continuously for fifty-three years. It was a sad day for Richmond.

There wasn't even a glimmer of hope for her future.

CHAPTER FIVE
The Dream

After the Byrd closed in 1982, I continued working for Neighborhood Theatres. From the Byrd, I moved on to the Westover, the Capitol, the National and finally, the Chesterfield Cinemas.

I learned how to manage a movie theatre. I learned how to keep controls on inventories, manage employees, and most importantly how to handle large crowds, most of which were friendly; some were not.

The job entailed long hours. I arrived early in the morning and left late in the evening, seven days a week. It wasn't exactly an exciting job for a young man with ambition, but I needed time to dream. I needed time to dream about how I was going to reopen the Byrd. And I needed to dream about how to keep her open and viable for many years to come.

But there was a lot to be done before the Byrd could be reopened.

Physically, the Byrd needed a lot of work. Almost everything in the theatre was worn out and in need of repair. The roof had been replaced ten years earlier, but was in bad shape. There were significant signs of a leaking roof, plaster damage and worse, falling pieces of the ceiling.

The entire balcony area had been closed off to the public for years because of the problem. Areas in the orchestra section needed to be roped off to protect patrons from the danger of falling plaster.

And although the Byrd seated over thirteen hundred patrons, only five to six hundred seats were available. The rest were in disrepair and roped off for a variety of safety reasons.

Mechanically, all of the HVAC systems worked, but they had been patched up so many times that it would take only the threat of a thunderstorm to shut things down. The concession counter was ugly and inefficient. The projectors and sound equipment were antiquated. In a nutshell, the Byrd Theatre was history.

We needed a plan.

Every idea had to be put on paper and needed a dollar amount assigned to it. Restoration cost money and money was hard to come by, especially for an old theatre with no patrons, that was hemorrhaging money, was costly to maintain, and was desperately in need of repair.

The Byrd was between a rock and a hard place. The single screen venue was much too large to exhibit first run movies profitably, but dividing her into multi-screens was physically and aesthetically impossible.

Maybe this is a good time to explain what "First Run" exhibition means. Neighborhood Theatres was a "First Run" exhibition chain of theatres. They only showed recently released new movies. Most theatre chains incorporate this policy of exhibition.

So, the first question one must ask is: "What is the process of acquiring the licensing agreement to exhibit a First Run Film? The first thing that happens is an invitation from the Hollywood Studio to view their film. In Richmond during the 1980s, there were only two major exhibitors; Neighborhood Theatres and United Artist Theatres. They pretty much split the town in half with the James River being the dividing line.

Once the exhibitors screen the film, the exhibitors offer a bid to exhibit the film in their theaters. It used to be that these bids were blind, meaning that the competing exhibitor didn't know what the other competing exhibitor bids were. This pretty much changed during the 1980s and it was because Disney wanted to continue this blind bid policy that the Byrd Theatre was able to show Disney films exclusively in 1990.

A typical bid for a licensing agreement for a first run film went something like this. I'll use the big Hollywood release *Jaws* as an example. Say the deposit is $100,000 per screen. The deposit is good faith money the studio holds in escrow. The terms over a sixteen week run are as follows: The first two weeks are split 90/10 over house expenses—the studio keeps ninety percent of the box office; the exhibitor keeps ten percent of the box office. This is the division of the take after the overhead or house expense has been accounted for; the second two weeks, 80/20 over house expenses. The third two weeks, 70/30 over house expenses; And so on until the sixteenth week, the exhibitor pays a flat thirty-five percent of the box office. Obviously, the exhibitor wants a long run because the longer the run, more of the box office receipts the exhibitor keeps.

Sixteen-week contract runs are common. This is probably the biggest reason for the transition from a single screen to a multi-screen operation.

Now on a film like *Jaws*, a theatre is full for a long time, way exceeding the contract time. But what happens when you show a "Blockbuster Flop" like *Ishtar*? What happens is you're stuck showing a film nobody wants to see for sixteen weeks. For a theatre like the Byrd, that's disastrous!

If you look at a seven-screen multi-theatre complex as an example. Two of the screens are larger seating, maybe five hundred to seven hundred patrons and the other screens are smaller seating as few as two hundred patrons. This was roughly the breakdown at the Ridge Cinema in the West End of Richmond. So, if you have a flop, you can just move the flop to a smaller screen. The Ridge Cinema was

Neighborhood Theatres' flagship theater through the 1990s. It was sad to see her torn down and replaced by a grocery store. Today, it's not unfamiliar to see twenty-plus screen operations.

In order for the Byrd to exhibit first run films competitively, it would need to add additional screens. But that would destroy the Byrd's beautiful interior and she would lose her charm.

I wasn't going to be the one responsible for that.

I needed a new concept.

My idea was to reproduce the programming of New York's Roxy Theatre.

It would be difficult—maybe impossible. I needed to find a success story and mimic it. The problem was that there were no large historic theatres making a profit in smaller markets like Richmond.

My other option was to find a variety of concepts and blend them all together to create my own incredible success story.

I was willing to compromise, if compromise was the solution. But I still needed to figure out what would be compromised?

I got plenty of advice on the matter:

"You don't need to show movies, people will pay just to see the place."

"Show the classics, after all, that's what they did when the Byrd was opened."

"Show the *Love Bug*; when they showed the *Love Bug*, they had lines wrapped around the block."

"You have to get new seats; no one over five feet tall can sit in those seats."

It was all generally good advice (especially the one about the seats), but here's the thing, none of those suggestions would sustain the Byrd for a week, much less a year or longer.

Timing is everything (another bit of good advice). After careful thought and consideration, I came up with a plan. The most important part of any plan is consistency. Start with a formula and stick with it.

This was my plan:

The Byrd Theatre was going to be a repertory movie theater that would feature live shows four times a year.

It would show some classic films, some second run films and some first run art films. We would have double bills at times and change movies as often as possible. Our means of advertising would be based on a calendar of events and shows, and to make certain our distribution cost would stay somewhat on a budget, we would run films recently shown by other theatres in markets close to Richmond.

The two theatres that came to mind were the Naro in Norfolk, Virginia, and the Vinegar Hill in Charlottesville, Virginia. Both theaters had similar programming and were successful! But, they were much smaller theatres with much lower overhead.

I would develop live performances four times a year to showcase Richmond's local talent. The shows would be vaudevillian by design, with inspiration taken from other live venues around the country.

But movies would have to be the mainstay for several reasons.

First and foremost, the Byrd didn't have a stage. Second, the Byrd was designed as a movie theater and as previously mentioned, consistency is essential. I didn't want the Byrd to break away from its scheduled programming or preempt movies for special one night shows.

But there would definitely be times in the calendar year that the movies wouldn't draw adequate attendance. In those cases, live shows would be the draw.

Getting started was a learning experience. The Byrd was closed and therefore had no audience to build from. The Byrd was in Carytown and Carytown was mostly dark (no lit storefronts) and boarded up in 1983.

During this time, Richmond was like most cities in the country. From the air, it looked like a big doughnut with developments in the suburbs and nothing happening downtown. This was logical, since most of the people were living in the suburbs. Reaganomics was the biggest play in turning this around. Most of the incentives for restoring downtown areas in the country came through Federal and State tax credits.

The Byrd's programming had to be varied.

Since the Byrd had no audience to begin with, I really had no idea as to what type of programming would work. I had to work from some assumptions, whether those assumptions were correct or not.

I assumed moviegoers would patronize the theatre twice a month. This assumption stayed true throughout my tenure. The price for movies had to be constant and for the most part. Customers could see a movie nightly at 7:15 p.m. and 9:45 p.m. The weekend matinees would always be open for attractions outside of the nightly movies.

At one time and for many years, the Byrd would show "Art Afternoons" for weekend matinees. During another time, the Byrd would have "Jazz Sunday Afternoons."

Single event promotions are expensive. Weekly promotions running over the course of several months would lower our advertising budget and increase our ability to succeed.

Jerry Cable and I worked together for years developing ideas of what to do with the Byrd Theatre.

As of September 1, 1983 I was no longer working for Neighborhood Theatres and worked solely for the Byrd Theatre Incorporated.

We planned a reopening for February 1984, but couldn't quite fit the pieces together to make that deadline. I learned more about business in those years with Cable than I learned in all of my years in college. Cable was methodical about everything he did—very smart.

After more planning and even more work, The Byrd Theatre reopened in April of 1984 with *Singin' in the Rain* starring Gene Kelly, Debbie Reynolds and Donald O'Connor. What a great opening film!

The parallels between the Byrd Theatre and *Singin' in the Rain* were unbelievable. *Singin' in the Rain* was about the transition to "Talkies" from the "Silent Era," and the Byrd was designed for the "Silent Era" only to open in 1928, then re-opened in 1984 to present "Talkies."

CHAPTER SIX
Restoration

While the Byrd Theatre was closed in the early 1980s, Rudisill, Cowardin, Barnett, I, and about a hundred of Richmond's local artisans, plumbers, electricians, carpenters, and contractors strove to rebuild, restore and reopen the Byrd Theatre.

I knew the restoration of historic properties was heavily scrutinized and generally cost much more than new construction of similar properties and it was difficult to find the high quality of artisans needed to complete the structural and cosmetic areas of the work.

The primary areas of interest for restoration were the seats, plaster and paint in the dome and balcony areas of the auditorium, and plaster and paint in the lobby, foyer and restrooms areas of the theatre.

The auditorium of the theatre was damaged primarily on the east wall due to the roof leak. The first thing to do was to replace the old existing roof. Although this was in the contract with the landlords, this was never done and wouldn't ever be done.

We needed to repair the roof and manage the leaks, otherwise all of the repairs to the plaster would be in vain, only to be under constant reparation. The leaks were managed by placing buckets and water diverting gutters.

The roof leaked like a sieve for twenty-five years, but the water seldom reached the plaster. Since only half of the Byrd was damaged by water, the restoration involved matching and blending the new plaster and paint with the old.

At this point, we need to look at the Byrd's design, particularly in the areas of heating, ventilation and air conditioning (HVAC.) To avoid creating drafts on customers, the air in the HVAC systems had to move from ceiling to floor. For air-conditioning, this air flow works efficiently and affordably, but for heating, it doesn't. Hot air rises; cold air falls.

If you look toward the dome areas of the Byrd, you can see black smudging on the round plaster vents. This was caused by coal dust moving through the system. During most of the Byrd's existence, the theatre used oil or gas to heat, but somewhere in time, probably during World War II, the Byrd was heated by coal, possibly due to the rationing of oil during the war.

For the new restoration, coal dust was mixed into the paint to match the old. Contractor bids to repair and paint the plaster work in the Byrd were as high as $500,000 -- unaffordable at the time.

So, Cowardin, Rudisill and I built the scaffolding necessary to reach the damaged areas. The grandchildren of the Byrd's original plasterers, William Saun and Gay Ligon, were hired to replace and repair the ornate plaster.

John Crocket, a local artisan, traversed the scaffolding every day for six months to paint a quarter of the Byrd's auditorium. Michelangelo could not have done a better job. All of the faux marbling in the lobby and foyer were painted by Crocket as well. By the way, John has a brother and his name is Davy Crocket.

The seats presented some real problems for several reasons. To begin, the air return vents are positioned underneath the seats. This made it difficult to reposition the seats and allow for more leg room. When the Byrd was built, the average height for men was around 5'6" and 5'1" for women. When the present day Byrd had a full house, packing them in like "sardines" was pretty much telling it like it was.

The seats were designed using spring coils much like sofas and beds are designed today. This design is comfortable for one's bottom, but an absolute nightmare on clothing. Quite often a spring would break loose and get lodged in someone's backside. The maintenance on those old seats was troublesome and expensive.

It cost way too much to replace the seats in 1984, but I still made plans. In the future, with the Byrd owned by a foundation under the 501(c)(3) umbrella, the seats could be restored in a manner not diminishing from the Theatre's beauty and seating capacity while allowing for modern comfort.

This could prove to be a challenge.

Here's a solution at a glance: Keep the original seats, standards and end caps. Replace the bottoms and backs with a thinner comfortable cushion. This would add more knee room and would take away the constant maintenance of always replacing broken springs.

The seats toward the back of the theatre are on tiers. It is difficult and expensive to reposition these seats, but this only encompasses the back few rows. The rest of the seats in the auditorium can be repositioned. The return vents run in the same direction as the aisles. So to reposition the vents would be difficult, but not impossible.

Aged concrete is one of the biggest obstacles. It's difficult to cut or drill into aged concrete, but repositioning the rows of seats would allow for more knee room. The Byrd would have slightly fewer seats, but the overall appearance would stay intact and ninety percent of the seats would be more comfortable for today's taller people.

Since the balcony is tiered, the only option for more comfortable seating would be to replace the seats and backs with a thinner spring-less cushion.

The antique concession counter is a beautiful piece of furniture. It's a display case purchased by Cable probably in the late 1970s when he was building the Tobacco Company Restaurant. The case came from an old drug store fountain area in New York City. The back bar came from the Gatsby's 1302 Restaurant in Shockoe Slip.

All of the antiques were in terrible shape and when they were placed in the Byrd for a trial look, they fell apart.

Gary Thomas of Governors Antiques restored all of the antiques to their former glory.

Most of the Neighborhood Theatres concession revenue was around thirty cents for every patron ticket sold. The Byrd's antique concession stand's revenue was around $1.80 per patron ticket sold; mostly because of my station design.

The Byrd's concession counter has four stations. Each station has its own popcorn, drinks, candies and cash drawer. The stand was so efficient that by the late 1980s, theatre owners were coming from all over the country just to check it out.

The stand is efficient in serving up to four hundred patrons. Above four hundred patrons and the stand became inefficient, but it never produced less than $1.10 per patron ticket sold.

Towards the middle to late 1990s the Byrd Theatre was drawing over ten thousand patrons a week. Even with those crowds, concession sales generated $1.10 per patron in revenue.

Concession sales were accounted for through inventory controls. Inventory controls were very tight until I vacated the Byrd at the end of 2005. Nelson Communications continued to operate the Byrd until the spring of 2007.

The rest rooms were another challenge, primarily because the marquee leaked. Unlike the auditorium roof leaks, the marquee leaks were manageable. The problem was that the drain lines leaked and caused the plaster on the ceilings and the interior walls of the restrooms to fall. Leak fixes were always temporary, so Rudisill, Cowardin and I all became good at plastering and painting.

Miles Rudisill kept the Byrd Theatre in pristine shape. From 1984 to 2007, Rudisill worked long days and nights to keep the seats, the plaster and paint in good repair -- almost to perfection.

He was constantly making repairs, fixing broken seats, and sewing torn curtains and fabric. Without Rudisill, the Byrd would have looked shabby and worn. But the Byrd always looked well-preserved and presentable.

I spared no expense to keep the Byrd in pristine shape. The carpet was replaced every three years. The antiques were rotated in and out for repairs. And most of the artisan work was done as it was done when the Byrd was originally built -- mostly using the same type of materials.

The mechanical systems were a nightmare to keep going.

At the time the Byrd reopened its doors in 1984, the furnace and air-conditioning were close to twenty years old. Although they were good systems, running them non-stop for that many years was hard on them. They were wearing out.

The air-conditioning was a Trane CentraVac system that used R-13 Freon which leaked and was obsolete. It was expensive and hard to obtain. Eventually, the only place we could get R-13 was from black market dealers.

The three-phase electric motors were always breaking down and difficult and expensive to rebuild or replace. The projectors were old and still burned carbon arc lamps to make the light. But the sound heads, gears, sprockets and lenses were all in good shape.

I give Gary Cowardin credit for keeping the Byrd projection, sound and lights operational. The organ and much of the mechanical systems, I credit to David Barnett.

Rudisill, Barnett and Cowardin and I worked hard to save the Byrd in the mid to late 1980s. But it's hard to credit any one individual for the Byrd's success in those years. We all worked well together as a group.

All in all, the Byrd was an expensive building to maintain and operate. The electric bill ran as high as $5,000 a month in the 1990s. The gas, water and sewage bills generally ran closer to $2,000 per month.

A big part of the expense was the twenty five percent utility tax levied by the city of Richmond on commercial properties.

The Byrd never had any of those services cut off for lack of payment, although it was close a few times.

The Mighty Wurlitzer

SPECIAL ENGAGEMENT
AN EXTRAORDINARY
EVENT

WINGS

Fanfare,

For 67 years, the Byrd Th...
most resplendent. Even now, wor...
dance lacking at the multi-plexes...
gital audio tape, the Byrd is Mozart...
The theater's uniqueness is not...
Often the best part of the evening is the...
organ rises from below floor level and L...
trade, house organist, belts out the Wur...
ter's big-wind sounds — and it's almost...
Eddie Weaver all over again. It's a little...
campy, like the flapper-girl costumes worn by...
the concessionaires — but then the camp is...
half the fun.
The other half is listening to a live...
performance with an instrument few today...
ever get to hear. Now, Richmonders who...
enjoy listening to the Wurlitzer when they go out can enjoy it when they say they...
The Virginia Theater Organ Society and the Byrd have conspired to release...
Byrd Sings," a compact disc of recordings made with the Wurlitzer.
Ron Rhode plays the instrument for the recording. Chuck Rhode...
vocals. The scores range from the Cavalleria Rusticana intermezzo to Tu...
"Over a Four-Leaf Clover." The CD is available at least music to Tu...
itself, of course, remains on Cary Street where, with any the music here, Th...
fortune, it will stay open for a long...

THE PIC...
THE PICTUR...

**Richmond's Historic
Byrd Theatre**

CHAPTER SEVEN
Live Presentations

With the Byrd's scheduled programming, there were times when live presentations could be exhibited without the interruption or preemption of already scheduled entertainment.

This was important—consistency was an absolute must. The Byrd would show films for two to three day runs. Sometimes a film would open a three day run and bomb the first day. In that case you bit the bullet and settled for an empty house. Nevertheless, we kept to the schedule.

The Byrd schedule was distributed on a two month printed calendar for the first five years. This type of calendar was successful at the Naro Theatre in Norfolk and the Vinegar Hill Theatre in Charlottesville. But the schedule was the biggest pain in the neck to produce, print and distribute.

Barnett, Rudisill and I would spend months making those calendars, always putting in all nighters before the press deadline. But it worked; at least the general consensus was that it worked.

There were problems with having a rigid calendar. The biggest was that it locked us in. This was great for your competition and distribution, but sometimes bad for the Byrd.

Quite often we would show films following the Naro in Norfolk.

We did this to cut down on film shipping costs. When the film finished playing at the Naro, someone from the Byrd would drive down to Norfolk and bring the film to the Byrd, basically for gas money.

But, if another theater hijacked the film between the Naro and the Byrd, as happened quite often, the Byrd would have to bring in a print from somewhere else. Once, the Byrd played *Gone with the Wind* and to keep with the schedule, the film was flown in from the West Coast, at a cost of four hundred dollars!

When you're only charging a couple of bucks for admission, it's hard to absorb that kind of a transportation expense. Fortunately, *Gone with the Wind* was a favorite and the house was always packed. In those cases, brisk concessions sales could make up the difference.

Another problem with keeping to a schedule was the competition. The Byrd's biggest movie competition in the late 1980s was not Blockbuster Video but the Westover dollar theatre.

Here's a prime example: the Byrd had *Crocodile Dundee* scheduled for a weekend run. The Westover presented the film two weeks before the Byrd. The results for the Westover were phenomenal— sellout crowds for two weeks! The results for the Byrd were dismal.

These were the two of the biggest reasons the Byrd eventually would drop her price and become a discount house. But this wouldn't happen until the early 1990s.

By 1986, open for a year, we had a good sense of when the Byrd was going to be seasonally busy or slow. The period just after Thanksgiving weekend, before Christmas Day, was three weeks of absolute death. There were Christmas parties and shopping, to occupy movie goers time. Generally, Blockbuster movies aren't released until Christmas Day.

Before the company could determine a remedy, the company had to know the rhyme or reason why.

Thanksgiving weekend was always busier for lots of reasons. Students are home from school with lots of free time on their hands, everyone is stuffed from eating too much turkey, and everyone is sick and tired of football and being around family. So, let's go see a movie!

Christmas day and the days after are busy at the theatres for all of the same reasons. Plus, Christmas day has always been one of the big Hollywood release days of the year; so again, let's go to the movies!

CHAPTER EIGHT
The Mighty Wurlitzer

During the silent era of movie presentation, the movies were anything but silent. In the beginning, silent films exhibited in Byrd-type theatres were often presented with the accompaniment of orchestras and grand theatre organs. Toward the latter years of the Silent Era, the orchestras got smaller and the theatre organs got bigger.

So when the Byrd opened its doors in 1928, the theatre boasted of housing one of the largest and most versatile theatre organs in the country. The Byrd's Mighty Wurlitzer could produce just about any sound effect imaginable; from birds to automobile engine and horn sounds, to wind and airplane sounds.

Unfortunately, most silent films presented today are accompanied by a single pianist, but in the 1920s it was quite a different story. The Byrd's programming in the mid-to-late 1980s presented over a dozen silent films with organ accompaniment.

The Byrd was lucky to have one of the most brilliant young organists, whose silent film compositions really brought silence in silent films to the heights of musical heaven in sound.

Lin Lunde had been a student of the legendary Eddie Weaver, but his ability to compose the many scores for the Byrd's silent films was pure talent. I often thought of Lunde's musical creations as so wonderful as to be compared to Mozart; Lunde possessed amazing talent.

During my tenure, the Byrd was fortunate to have some great organists. To start in the mid 1980s with Lin Lunde and then end my tenure in the mid 2000s with Bob Gulledge was quite an honor. For such a small town, Richmond had a lot of organ talent.

Just about every weekend, the Virginia Theatre Organ Society (VTOS) organ crew would meet in the theatre and spend hours working to repair and maintain the Byrd's Mighty Wurlitzer Theatre Organ. All of the work was done pro bono, so the only real expense to the Byrd was the organist playing evening shows on weekends..

Between 1984 and 2007, the Byrd hosted some fine organists. In order of their appearance were: Lin Lunde, James Hughes, Bob Lent, and Bob Gulledge. All of the organists, except for James Hughes, were theatre organ trained. Lin Lunde and Bob Gulledge had been students of the great Eddie Weaver, who made a few guest appearances in the late 1980s.

I had admiration for all of the organists who played at the Byrd, although Lin Lunde had a unique brilliance in silent film accompaniment. All of them had great stage presence and showmanship, and most could make the necessary temporary organ repairs or adjustments to keep things going on schedule. Between the organists, Barnett and the VTOS, the Byrd's Mighty Wurlitzer sounded pretty good in the late 1980s and 1990s and well into the 2000s.

There were always good stories of things happening at the Byrd. One memorable night would be forever remembered as the night of the "Impromptu Lunde Concert."

CHAPTER NINE
The Show Must Go On!

In the late 1980s the Byrd was consistent in having two shows a night: the early show starting at 7:15 p.m. and the later show starting at 9:45 p.m. For the most part, the early show started on time, but the later show sometimes kicked off a little late.

But, if we advertised a 10:00 p.m. showing, our attendance for that show would be half of what it would be if the show was advertised at 9:45 p.m. If the running time of the movie was two hours or less, we could most often start the shows on time, that is at 7:15 p.m. and 10:00 p.m.

Generally, the movies would be shipped from the distributor on Thursday night for a Friday night opening. So, every Friday, the projectionist would arrive around noon and "make the film up." "Making a film up" means checking it in, inspecting it, splicing reels together, and transferring the film from shipping reels to the better made house reels. This preparation is to ensure that the film is in presentable shape and to help ensure a good screening.

Quite often the Byrd would receive films in bad, non-presentable condition as on one snowy Friday morning in January 1987. The film we received was in such poor shape, with so many bad splices and missing scenes, that the musical would have been better shown and heard with the sound turned off. This was a two hour film that had been cut and spliced into a film with a running time of under an hour.

In a case like this, I would have to scramble to get a new print, have it shipped, and have it made up, all before show time. This happened often, but generally it wasn't snowing and the film wasn't in such bad shape.

A good projectionist, like Bill Enos, could work miracles and make almost anything presentable enough to run, but not in this case. The search was on.

We found a film and it was scheduled to arrive in Richmond on the 5:00 p.m. bus. This would give Enos plenty of time to ready the film for a 7:15 showing.

At 5:15, Rudisill is at the bus station, all of the busses are in, and there is no film. Rudisill calls me from a pay phone. I relay the tracking information.

The film missed its first bus. And the bus that the film did make is now delayed because of the snow and won't arrive until 7:00.

We scrambled to come up with a plan.

Lunde will start playing right at 7:15 and instead of playing for ten minutes as usual, he will play until the Byrd logo appears on the curtain, signaling that Enos is ready to start the film.

When the film arrives at the bus station, Rudisill will call the theatre for a heads up, grab the film, and drive it to the Byrd. Like passing a baton in a relay race, Rudisill will hand the film off to an usher who will haul it up four flights to the projection room so Enos can signal Lunde to finish up. Enos will thread the first reel and the show will start.

It was a great plan.

But at 7:15, Rudisill was still waiting at the bus station. The bus finally rolled into the station at 7:25. Rudisill called the theatre, grabbed the film and headed off to the Byrd.

Navigating through snow and sleet, through a gauntlet of pothole-filled streets, Rudisill makes his way to the Byrd Theatre in record time!

Meanwhile, back at the Byrd, Lunde was twenty-five minutes into his ten-minute pre-show organ spot.

Anyone who regularly patronized the Byrd Theatre knew Lunde always opened with Irving Berlin's, *There's No Business Like Show Business*. Then he moved on to another musical number before closing with a number from the movie the Byrd was presenting that evening.

Twenty-five minutes into this and Lunde was probably hoping the Byrd was playing *Annie Get Your Gun*, and please shoot me and take me out of this misery!

When the Byrd Logo finally appeared on the screen, Lunde had played for forty minutes, composed several new operas, and lost about ten pounds.

Through it all, Lunde really showed his genius; he played all of this from memory. Lunde didn't use sheet music (he thought it looked unprofessional.) He didn't need it. Lunde made everything difficult look easy.

I mentioned to Lunde a little later, "Thanks Lin! That was a great job! I think that there may be a little something extra in your Christmas stocking this year for a job well done!" Ain't life grand?

Lunde's greatest gift was his talent to compose theatre organ accompaniment for silent films. Lunde was a genius; like Mozart, his manuscripts were written in free hand and were comprised mainly of chicken scratches no one else could make heads or tails of.

He viewed *Wings*, the first Academy Award winner for Best Picture in 1929 once, maybe twice; and then composed one of the most incredible accompaniments believable. The Byrd presented *Wings* several times in the 1980s—always to a sold out and appreciative crowd.

The Byrd would often have pre-movie entertainment. That is, entertainment other than just the organist; but, most often the organist was involved to some degree or another. All of the entertainment was planned and was actually well thought through, but seldom rehearsed.

Once, around Halloween for the 1925 silent film *Phantom of the Opera*, we thought of a unique way of introducing Lunde. Instead of having Lunde riding the organ console up to center stage from the bowels of the theatre as usual, the thought was instead to have him enter by means of a coffin.

That's right—a coffin carrying Lunde would be ushered down an aisle by six pallbearers and placed on the lip of the stage left of the organ. From that point, Lunde would raise the coffin lid, climb out, mount the rising Mighty Wurlitzer console, play for five to ten minutes, and then lower to stage level to accompany the film, which in this case ran about 107 minutes.

Now, if there had been time for at least one rehearsal, we felt certain things would have gone a bit smoother. Actually, to the audience, most of the Byrd's shows looked rehearsed and flawlessly presented; a peek behind the scenes revealed an entirely different perspective.

I give credit to a lot of the early sets and props to the workshop of Gary Goerss, whose shop was next door to the Byrd. It was there that an 1850s style wooden coffin was built to absolute perfection. The coffin construction was not the problem.

Rehearsal would have revealed that the aisles narrowed from the back of the auditorium to the stage. At the back of the auditorium; the aisles are wider than they are towards the front of the auditorium; actually two feet wider. So, when six good-sized fellows carry a body-filled coffin down an ever-narrowing aisle, something is going to go amiss.

And usually that something amiss happens on opening night; doesn't go unnoticed, and always happens at the most inopportune time.

In the midst of the thunder and the lightning special effects by

Gary Cowardin, six volunteers (as usual, recruited "British Navy Style" from the audience) pallbearers carrying Lunde down the aisle for the first time start to run out of room. With no room to walk and with the coffin beginning to pitch and list as a ship on a stormy sea, panic starts to break out and then all hell breaks loose!

Lunde hears, "I'm dropping him, I'm dropping him," and the ladies sitting next to the aisles start sharing their seats with the pallbearers; that's not a good way to begin a show!

To make things worse, the special effects quit, the room goes dead silent and now the audience is tuned in to what's happening. Yes, there were some high pitched screams, mostly from Lunde; and a few four letter words invented, you know, words like "GOLF," but by some miraculous force, Lunde did make it to the stage; maybe a little shaken, but not stirred, and very much alive.

And as one can always count on, Lunde put on one "hell of a show" that night. Lunde's Christmas stocking just got filled with a little something special.

Now the business death in December has always been attributed to a lot of reasons, but it's mostly because everyone is getting into the holiday spirit of spending money.

You've got Christmas shopping, Christmas parties, Christmas music and Christmas parades. I know the Twelve Days of Christmas begin on Christmas day, but by the time Christmas day actually arrives, everyone is really ready to be over with Christmas much less face another twelve days of it.

So the Byrd, with all of her heartfelt spirit, got into the commercial spirit. Thus, the Christmas Celebration was born!

The first Christmas Celebrations were small in comparison to the latter ones of the late 1980s. The shows always preceded the movies and the movies were always Christmas oriented.

Usually the movies selected were *Miracle on 34th Street* or a double bill of, *It's a Wonderful Life* and *The Bells of St. Mary's*.

It's a Wonderful Life is an obvious choice, but a lot of folks wonder why *The Bells of St. Mary's* was always paired with it. The reason is simple; there is a scene in which Jimmy Stewart is running through the snowy streets of Bedford Falls when the camera catches the marquee of the town theater. *The Bells of St. Mary's* is showing. That brief shot always got a big round of applause.

The pre-show entertainment is what really made the early Christmas Celebrations fun shows. The organist would rise to center stage, play a few warm-up numbers, take a bow and then lower the organ to the orchestra level.

Back in 1984, the orchestra pit was covered, so the organist's head was level with the stage-covered orchestra pit. The spotlight would turn to the harp alcove where vocalist Chuck Rhode would sing one song and then the curtain would rise for sing-a-longs. There would always be one non-secular song (usually *O Holy Night*) but for the most part the organist tried to stay with a secular fare.

Also, the Christmas Celebration always made good use of the piano alcove. David Newman was my favorite Byrd pianist. Newman by trade was a piano tuner and set builder. Later, in 1987 when the Byrdettes made their second appearance in the 1987 Christmas show, Newman made the wood cutout Byrdettes for the marquee. Beautifully handmade and hand painted, those wooden Byrdettes really classed up the old Byrd Theatre marquee.

Not everyone knew this, but the Byrd's piano didn't need a pianist. The keys could move on their own, pneumatically controlled from the theatre organ's console. It was the organist who was actually playing the piano. This was a favorite skit of Lunde and a practical joke to play on Newman. When Newman stood to take a bow, for his marvelous playing, the piano would keep playing even though his hands were a good distance from the keys.

The Byrd Theatre often made use of sing-a-longs as pre show entertainment. Everyone wanted the bouncing ball sing-a-longs famous in the 1940s and '50s. The problem was that the bouncing ball sing-a-longs were not designed for theatre organ accompaniment.

So, the Byrd would simply turn off the sound track and Lunde would score an original accompaniment for it. These were always fun!

Other pre show entertainment complementing feature film presentations were cartoons. Some of the best cartoons featured Bugs Bunny, Daffy Duck, Porky Pig, Tweety and the Road Runner by Warner Brothers Animation. Fortunately, this was a time when Warner Brothers was restoring all of their vintage cartoons, so the prints were pristine.

CHAPTER TEN
Easter Show and the Byrdettes

The first Christmas Celebrations in December of 1984 and 1985 were huge successes. The original shows were presented for only one weekend and lasted only fifteen minutes, but the timing was perfect.

The Christmas show helped the Byrd Theatre out when there was normally a slowdown in business and it opened up some great ideas for future shows. So, in January 1986, the Byrd started planning its first Easter Show and the world premiere of the Byrdettes.

I now had the showmanship "bug." As Lin Lunde would play before every weekend show, *There's No Business Like Show Business*.

I started seeing as many theatrical productions as possible. Rudisill and I would travel to New York City. We would see shows at Radio City Music Hall and the Metropolitan Opera House. Most often, we would take the train from Richmond, Virginia to Hoboken, New Jersey and then the Port Authority Trans-Hudson (PATH) into New York City. Staying in Hoboken was a lot cheaper than staying in the city and the PATH made it only a New York minute from Manhattan.

This would be my first experience to actually see the Radio City Music Hall Rockettes live. My only other exposure was in the library of Miles Rudisill.

The Rockettes became famous as the Roxyettes at the famed Roxy Theatre in New York City back in the 1920s. When Samuel L. Rothafel, aka "Roxy," moved to the Radio City Music Hall in 1932, he moved the Roxyettes with him and renamed them the Rockettes. The Rockettes are a 36-girl synchronized line of dancers. Each dancer is roughly the same height and weight and look. The Rockettes are all professionally trained in jazz, tap, and ballet. To see the Rockettes perform on the stage of the Radio City Music Hall is an experience in life everyone should enjoy.

In preparation for the Byrd's 1986 Easter Show, I needed to find a director. The director not only needed to be a theatrical stage director, but a choreographer as well.

There were several good theater companies in Richmond in 1986. There was the Theater of Virginia, Theatre IV, The Barksdale Dinner Theater, The Haymarket Dinner Theater, and The Swift Creek Mill Playhouse. Of those, I looked at two very good directors: Bev Appleton from The Haymarket and Randy Strawderman from The Barksdale.

My visit to the Barksdale Theater and their performance of *Joseph and the Amazing Technicolor Dreamcoat* moved my decision in favor of choosing Strawderman to direct the Byrd's first Easter show. Both directors were well-educated and experienced in professional theater, but Strawderman had a real flair and was an exceptional choreographer.

Most would say that producing a live show at the Byrd Theatre was impossible, and most people would be absolutely right. The Byrd theatre had no stage, no green rooms, and no dressing rooms. Did I mention it didn't have a stage?

Not having a stage also meant having no lights or sound system, definitely two necessities for a live show.

What the Byrd had was a forty foot wide sliver of an apron that extended twelve feet in front of the proscenium curtain. Between the curtain and the fixed screen was a space of about two feet. Strawderman, Rudisill, Cowardin and I had to use all our creativity if we wanted to stage a show at the Byrd.

In our minds, the Byrd Theatre had three performance areas. The apron could provide a dance area for the Byrdettes, as long as a trap door could be made to cover the organ console elevator shaft when the organ was not in use. The other two areas were the piano alcove and harp alcove. Both areas could be accessed through trap doors under the alcoves behind the two exit curtains towards the front of the stage.

The Byrd Theatre had a tradition of opening every weekend movie with a short performance by the theatre organist. This was necessary to allow patrons at the concession stand and patrons purchasing tickets time to find seats.

Lin Lunde always said one of the most entertaining aspects of the theatre organ was the elevator used to bring the organ up to stage level and then back down again. This was the signal to all of the patrons that the show was about to begin.

The theatre organ did take up space in the middle of the Byrd's small stage. To remedy this, I hired the Blankenship family contractors to build a swinging trap door to cover the theatre organ opening once the organist performance was finished. This had to be done with efficiency so all of the shows could be staged in a timely fashion.

The key to set construction in any theatre application is to "beef up" everything. The Blankenships made the trap doors strong enough to support elephants, yet they could be swung into position with the greatest of ease. Most of the time, Lunde handled the trap doors by himself.

The first couple of shows at the Byrd were staged in vaudevillian fashion. Vaudeville was a style of presenting a variety of many entertainments within one stage setting. The key to having a successful vaudevillian show is to conduct a smooth running show with no stops. Sets and performers have to be able to move in and out of a single space smoothly. Under the most favorable vaudevillian conditions, the stage has room allowed for curtains and drops to help petition stage areas in order to continuously introduce new acts.

There is nothing worse than having to stop a show, break down one set and replace it with another set, every time you change entertainment.

We never had to worry about that at the Byrd. We had no stage, so not having to build sets and drops kept the stage costs to a minimum. On the other hand, in order to provide for smooth running continuous entertainment, we had to create multiple stages. So, instead of building sets and drops, we created stages.

As I mentioned before, the Byrd had three stages in her two alcoves and one apron. Spot lights and blackouts helped the Byrd's shows to move seamlessly.

Radio City Music Hall has thirty-six Rockettes performing synchronized dance movements across a 120-foot wide stage. The stage is as deep as it is wide and uses the same elevator technology found on aircraft carriers. All of the Rockettes are between 5'8" and 5'10," with an average weight of 120 pounds.

New York is a big entertainment city with a lot of talent. Richmond, VA is not New York City. We did not have the Rockettes, but Richmond did have the Byrdettes.

Often called Randy Strawderman's Byrdettes; the Byrdettes were conceived by me, but brought to life by Strawderman. The Byrd couldn't copy the Rockettes in size and numbers, but the Byrdettes were far prettier and much more talented. They had to be. The average distance between the Rockettes and the Radio City's audience is one hundred-fifty feet; at the Byrd, the distance is just forty-five feet. The Byrdettes height ran from 5'3" to 5'8" with varying weights.

Since a chorus line is all about synchronizations and similar appearances, there had to be some manipulation of Jan Paxton's costume designs. There were rumors of tape being used in various places to keep certain body parts in alignment with the other girl's body parts. The duct tape tale is just a myth, but there were a lot of shadows created using a lot of makeup.

How do you make a 5'3" Byrdette appear the same height as a 5'8" Byrdette?

The two methods Paxton used were shoe heel height and costume cut. Some of the Byrdettes were dancing in one inch heels and others were dancing in three inch heels. Some of the costumes were tailored with lower cleavage lines (not a bad thing) and some were tailored with higher hip lines (again not a bad thing). The chorus line was arranged with the shorter Byrdettes on the ends of the line and the taller dancers set toward the center of the line.

Changing costumes in makeshift dressing rooms was a stage manager's nightmare. Luckily, the Byrd had a good one in Mary Sue Carroll.

The Byrdettes looked and performed beautifully. Even though the inaugural 1986 Byrdettes Easter show opened to mixed reviews from critics, it was a huge financial success. Richmonders flocked in great numbers to see the Byrdettes.

The Byrd started to find its niche. With repertory showings of movies and then live shows four times a year, we were beginning to think we had a shot at keeping the Byrd open, alive, and well. Our next big show with the Byrdettes would be the 1986 Christmas Celebration!

Randy Strawderman wasn't just a director and choreographer, but a true impresario. He never had a written script to follow; everything at the Byrd was new and created from scratch. Besides the obvious handicaps the Byrd suffered from, lacking a stage, etc., Strawderman faced difficulty in finding talented performers.

Filling a stage with talented performers from the Richmond area was difficult, especially trying to fill a chorus line. He needed to find twelve experienced, talented, well studied, professional dancers. And on top of that, all twelve Byrdettes and alternates had to perform on the same synchronized level, in unison, as if they were all one unit.

I've never met an impresario with Strawderman's work ethic. Strawderman was brilliant, but his genius came from hard work.

The Mighty Wurlitzer

SPECIAL ENGAGEMENT
AN EXTRAORDINARY
EVENT

WINGS

BYRD SINCE 1928

ADMIT ONE   ANY REGULAR

ADMIT ONE   ANY REGULAR

ADMIT ONE   ANY REGULAR

VIP

ADMIT ONE   ANY RE
VIP   OR SP
PASS   BYR

Fanfare, Ple

For 67 years, the Byrd The
most resplendent. Even now, work
radiance lacking at the multi-plexes.
digital audio tape; the Byrd is Mozart
The theater's uniqueness is not
Often the best part of the evening is the m
organ rises from below floor level and
blonde, house organist, belts out the Wurlitzer's big-wind sounds — and it's
Eddie Weaver all over again. It's a
campy, like the flapper-girl costumes worn by
the concessionaires — but then the camp is
half the fun.

The other half is listening to a live
performance with an instrument few today
ever get to hear. Now, Richmonders who
enjoy listening to the Wurlitzer when they go out can enjoy it when they stay home
The Virginia Theater Organ Society and the Byrd have conspired to release "T
Byrd Sings," a compact disc of recordings made with the Wurlitzer
Ron Rhode plays the instrument for the recording; Chuck Rhode
vocals. The scores range from the Cavalleria Rusticana intermezzo to "In
Over a Four-Leaf Clover." The CD is available at local music stores
itself, of course, remains on Cary Str
fortune, it will stay open for a long

THE PIC
THE PICTURE

**Richmond's Historic
Byrd Theatre**

CHAPTER ELEVEN

Critics: You can't survive without them.

Anyone crazy enough to try to save a dying movie theatre should receive praise, and all the praise the Byrd was getting was truly welcome. Reviews of the shows meant the most to me. Because of the live shows and the great reviews, we at the Byrd would constantly strive for entertainment perfection and in doing so would help the Byrd stand alone and thrive.

The two main critics in the Richmond newspapers during the 1980s were Carole Kass and Roy Proctor.

Kass was the movie critic for the *Richmond Times-Dispatch* and Proctor was the theater critic for the *Richmond News Leader*. Both were seasoned writers, knowledgeable in their field and well-respected both nationally and in the Richmond area.

Film reviews were out of my hands since all of the movies were produced in Hollywood or elsewhere. Throughout my tenure, I never claimed to be a connoisseur of film. All of the second run films were booked according to the film's performance in other parts of the country in similar markets.

The first-run art films we screened were bigger risks, but fortunately I had Kass in my corner. First-run art films were always subjected to local reviews and Kass's personal policy was to never give a bad review. She believed any film in whole or in part could contribute in some way to someone's life.

Kass would walk out of a screening, asking me on the way to the door, "Do I have to sit through this anymore?"

And even though I knew Kass's opinion of the film, the review in the next morning's paper was always written to, let us say, entice movie goers to the Byrd. Kass was a good friend of the Byrd for a long time.

The critiques of the stage presentations were in my hands and the productions had to be professionally staged. If they were not, poor reviews could damage our bottom line at the box office. And when the Byrd was fighting just to stay alive, a bad review could cause irreparable financial damage and shut down the theater.

All of the value added entertainment was necessary. It was essential to present the best shows possible. The Byrd Theatre's long-standing reputation as the "Showplace of Virginia" was a huge responsibility to uphold.

The bigger shows at the Byrd were always difficult to finance. Most were paid for using different partnerships, which helped minimize the risk and the damage a poorly reviewed show could cause. Fortunately, the majority of the productions at the Byrd were never critically or financially unsuccessful; most received glowing reviews and, at the least, broke even financially.

All stage presentations were first developed on paper in the form of a prospectus. A good prospectus had realistic numbers on ticket sales and exaggerated numbers on expenses; therefore, most shows would show a breakeven on the prospectus. From the prospectus, you can budget your advertising, delegate responsibilities, and make changes to enhance the show, but the overall expenses could not exceed the expenses on the prospectus.

As long as we sold the right number of seats, the show would at least break even. Cost overruns can cause serious problems and are often due to poor planning and poor execution.

'A Christmas Celebration' is a crowd-pleaser

STAGE REVIEW
By Roy Proctor
News Leader arts editor

"A Christmas Celebration," which opened last night at the festively decorated Byrd Theater, defies easy classification. It's a 40-minute stage show, but it's just as much an audience show. It's part review, part vaudeville, part sing-a-long, part scaled-down Rockettes.

It celebrates Christmas, as does the feature-film classic, "Miracle on 34th Street," that follows it. Just as important, it celebrates a grand old movie palace and revives the pre-movie revue tradition that thrived in the 1930s and 1940s.

Above all, "A Christmas Celebration' is warm. Last night's near capacity audience saw to that. From great grannies to babies in arm, 1219 people poured into the 1360-seat Byrd primed to have a good time-and have a good time they did.

The festivities begin with organist Lin Lunde rising out of the stage floor to make merry at the console of the Byrd's Mighty Wurlitzer. Then lyric tenor Chuck Rhode sings two pop-Christmas numbers from the Byrd's harp alcove while Lunde, still at the Wurlitzer, and pianist David Newman, in the piano alcove, accompany him.

Now, it's sing-a-long time, with Lunde at the organ, lyrics projected on the screen and the audience joining in like redeemed Baptist on the last night of revival week, even though the songs are secular. Next up is David Hirschey, described in the program as a "master juggler," but he's just as much a master comedian.

At one point, the skinny, relaxed Hirschi is turning three

cascading balls into a visual equivalent of a horse race. At another, he keeps a ping-pong-ball, a bowling ball and a model of a "man-eating shark" in the air with ease. He's a charmer.

The finale is provided by choreographer Randy Strawderman's 12 high kicking Byrdettes, who perform a Charleston number and then launch into a traditional kick rouser from "Babes in Toyland" while outfitted in a lot of white fur, a lot of skin and a little red.

It's easy to pick nits with "A Christmas Celebration." The music is Christmasy but unrelentingly secular. Rhode, who is a celestial voice, should be turned loose on a song like "O Holy Night" to provide depth, more variety and the hush the show otherwise lacks.

Strawderman's Byrdettes know just what to do when they're on the stage-and they do it with pizazz-but more ingenuity is in order to get them on and off. And why have Newman playing that piano during Rhode's solos if its sound is completely eclipsed by Lunde's organ?

Nonetheless, "A Christmas Celebration" is a big crowd-Pleaser-and justifiable so. It's special and you feel special experiencing it. It's the longest and most ambitious stage show the Byrd management has attempted since the theater was restored and reopened several years ago.

And technically this show's enhanced sound and lighting systems make it a considerable improvement over the 20-minute Easter revue that introduced the Byrdettes last spring.

The Byrd has a long way to go in reclaiming its stage, most of which is still blocked by the stationary screen, and in making other strides in its staging capability, but "A Christmas Celebration" is a significant step in the right direction it will be repeated tonight at 8 o'clock and tomorrow at 3 and 8 p.m.

"A Christmas Celebration," a 40-minute stage show preceding a Bugs Bunny cartoon and the feature film. "Miracle on 34th Street." at the Byrd Theatre again tonight at 8 o'clock and tomorrow at 3 and 8 p.m. Directed by Duane Nelson; choreographed by Randy Strawderman; lighting by David Campbell; costumes by Jann Paxton.

Featuring organist Lin Lunde, lyric tenor Chuck Rhode, pianist David Newman, juggler David Hirschi and the Byrdettes. A chorus line consisting of Katheine Smith, Lisa Jackson, Stephanie Miller, Teresa Adams, Tanya Moring, Kristy Pierce, Marcia McCowan, Christy Roberts, Becky Weiss, Deborah Arenstein, Elizabeth Yavich and Deborah Wallace.

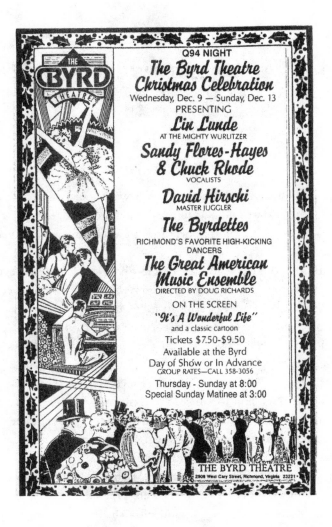

Q94 NIGHT

The Byrd Theatre Christmas Celebration

Wednesday, Dec. 9 — Sunday, Dec. 13

PRESENTING

Lin Lunde
AT THE MIGHTY WURLITZER

Sandy Flores-Hayes & Chuck Rhode
VOCALISTS

David Hirschi
MASTER JUGGLER

The Byrdettes
RICHMOND'S FAVORITE HIGH-KICKING DANCERS

The Great American Music Ensemble
DIRECTED BY DOUG RICHARDS

ON THE SCREEN

"It's A Wonderful Life"
and a classic cartoon

Tickets $7.50-$9.50

Available at the Byrd
Day of Show or In Advance
GROUP RATES—CALL 358-3056

Thursday - Sunday at 8:00
Special Sunday Matinee at 3:00

THE BYRD THEATRE
2908 West Cary Street, Richmond, Virginia 23221

CHAPTER TWELVE

The Real Deal: The Christmas Celebrations of
1987 and 1988

The Christmas Celebration of 1986 was so successful that the only direction to go was probably down. So, in 1986 I started work early on what would become an even bigger and better Christmas Celebration for 1987.

The Byrd would forego the Easter Show in 1987 for several reasons. One reason being that springtime in Richmond proved to be a difficult time to get patrons to move inside when the weather was so nice outside. Second, I needed the time to design and plan the building for a new stage. In order to produce better shows, the Byrd needed a stage.

There were a lot of difficulties in redeveloping the stage at the Byrd Theatre. First and foremost, the Byrd really never had a stage to begin with. Up until 1953, the time when Cinemascope was introduced, the stage consisted of two doors within a proscenium arch that masked the 15' x 20' projection screen.

This was the size of the screen Americans had seen their movies on since the late 1920s. The two doors were probably there to provide access to entertainers going on and off a shallow stage or perhaps used by the manager to introduce the feature film presentation at the time.

The screen position at this time was four feet from the back wall of the theatre and we know of only one photo showing a curtain hiding the screen with the doors visible on both sides. The screen was probably fixed in position.

On the Byrd's blueprints, the theatre was designed for silent film presentations, so on opening day, with the showing of *Waterfront* a talkie, there had to be some room for loudspeakers as well. They may have been placed in the orchestra pit or on both sides of the orchestra pit, possibly behind the screen as is the practice today, but we're not sure.

Since wide screens were available in the late 1920s, more than likely changes from the 12' x 12' screen shown on the blue prints were made before the Byrd opened in 1929.

But in 1953 Cinemascope changed everything for movie-going audiences. When the Byrd was reopened in 1984, a cinemascope size screen was still in place. In order to facilitate the 36' wide by 16' tall screen, it had been necessary to build scaffolding in front of the smaller proscenium arch with the two doors to support the large screen. This was a massive stationary perforated screen and three large loudspeakers were positioned behind the screen for sound.

Unfortunately, in 1953 there wasn't room for the scaffolding to support the screen and openings were punched through the inner proscenium arch to facilitate the scaffolding. So, any hopes of saving the inner proscenium were abandoned; it was severely damaged.

The plan to redevelop the Byrd's stage, in thought, was simple: replace the existing screen with one that could be rigged to hoist upwards above the stage and out of sight, remove the smaller proscenium arch to allow room for the stage, place the speakers on casters for easy removal, and achieve all of this without missing a single movie show. When the Byrd opened with the 1987 Christmas Celebration, the new stage would be a complete surprise to the audience.

The first thing I did was to solicit help from two of Richmond's theatrical talents, Reid Pierce, a licensed contractor with prominence in stage construction and theatrical staging and Robert Forman, stage manager and one of the original developers of the stage at the Carpenter Center for the Performing Arts. Both gentlemen performed stage transformations around the country and are still highly respected in their fields.

In the 1970s and 1980s, many old movie palaces were transformed into respected theatrical staging venues. The Carpenter Center, originally the Loews Theater in Richmond, is a prime example of a once old movie palace transformed into a modern performing arts center. Today, the Carpenter Theatre at Center Stage is home to the Richmond Symphony, the Richmond Ballet, The Virginia Opera, and many other companies..

One major difference was that the Byrd didn't have the financial resources to complete such a stage redevelopment. The stage at the Carpenter Center cost millions of dollars to build and the old Loews already had a stage and dressing rooms.

The goal was to build a simple stage to facilitate small shows and musical revues. In some spaces, this is called a black box theater.

A black box theater by definition is a simple, somewhat unadorned performance space used for experimental theater. The difference at the Byrd was that the space could be lighted and rigged and the sound system could be brought in according to the needs of the show. Although this meant bringing in rented lights, some rigging, and rented sound for every show, this also meant that the actual stage could be developed for a fraction of the initial costs for a well equipped stage.

So, even though the Byrd's stage building cost would be down, the production costs would be up. But this strategy was still an absolute necessity. Apart from the initial cost of the Byrd, $270,000 in 1982, the owners of the Byrd spent little if anything on the restoration of the building, on the upkeep of the building, or on the operations of the building for the twenty-five years they were the owners.

The majority of the financial risks taken at the Byrd were shouldered by Cable and myself between 1984 and 1989, and then from 1990 to 2007 by me alone. That was a tremendous burden!

Planning for the stage redevelopment took over a year. The actual construction was done two weeks before the opening of the 1987 Christmas Celebration. Planning the 1987 Christmas Celebration took about six months, with pre-production two months out, and production three days before opening. The set paint was still a little wet opening night.

The stage redevelopment started by first constructing a temporary wooden frame for the present screen, that had been in place for over thirty years. The screen was placed on the frame, temporarily hung in front of the raised gold curtain and the speakers placed as close behind the screen as possible.

Then, a heavy gauged plastic curtain was hung from ceiling to floor between the screen/speakers and the inner proscenium arch to help contain construction dust. All of this allowed workers to carefully dismantle the scaffolding and to allow enough room to begin demolition of the inner proscenium.

The inner proscenium, although severely damaged in 1953, was still attached in mortar and stone. Dismantling the inner proscenium took a week, done at night and carefully so as not to damage anything the Byrd would need in the future. In other words, sledgehammers were slung and swung with great care so as not to cause much flying debris.

The work reminded me of being at a crab house hammering claws for crab pickings. A big mess! Throughout the entire process, the audience had no idea a new stage was soon to be unveiled; the Byrd never missed a show.

For the first time in history, The Christmas Celebration was staged around the live music of Doug Richards and the Great American Music Ensemble. The idea was to present certain compositions from Duke Ellington's Nutcracker Suite which Ellington performed at

New York's Cotton Club in 1929. The only place Richards could find these recordings was on scratchy old 78 RPM records dating back to late 1929.

This is where Doug Richards is brilliant. He transcribed from the recordings and copied all of the handwritten sheet music for his fifteen piece orchestra. If you were fortunate to have heard the incredible sounds produced on the Byrd's stage in 1987 and 1988, you would have realized why Doug Richards and his Great American Music Ensemble have won so many Kennedy Center Awards.

While the stage was being built, Richards was busy transcribing in one part of the city while Melanie Snyder was busy choreographing the Byrdettes on a rehearsal stage in another part of the city.

Meanwhile, not too far away at a warehouse owned by Virginia Commonwealth University, the first set for the new stage and the 1987 Christmas Celebration was being built. Ron Keller, VCU Professor and set designer extraordinaire, was the man behind the designs of all the sets and scenes for the 1987 and 1988 Christmas Celebrations.

The idea for the 1987 set design came from Jean Cocteau's 1946 movie *Beauty and the Beast*. The bandstand set was designed to allow for a fireplace fantasy centered on a chimney with a stuck Santa Claus and revolving ballerinas, molded into the mantelpiece columns, that would come to life only on Christmas Celebration nights. *Take a breath; that was a long sentence.*

It was really cool! And the funny thing was that the set went onto the new stage the night before opening night. The dress rehearsal was performed on an unpainted set the day of opening night.

The set was so well designed that the movie sound speakers hung just inches over the set and the band's musicians couldn't enter the set until after the speakers were flown. The three speaker's weight was in excess of two tons, but as with everything else in the Byrd, the "I" beams used to support them probably could have held ten times that weight.

I was not concerned as much with dead weight, but with torque and tensile strength from moving weight. To avoid taking chances, I had a structural engineer test, approve and certify the structural integrity of the stage house, all of the rigging and all of the blocks and cables.

The 1987 Christmas Celebration was well-planned, but didn't really come together until opening night. This is a testament to the Byrd's Theatrical Staging Company, but especially to one of my first "Concessionaires," turned producer, Mary Burruss.

I can't say enough wonderful things about Mary Burruss. When she wasn't attending Virginia Commonwealth University as a full-time Fashion Marketing student, she was helping me open and manage the Byrd. Her responsibilities included concession counter staffing; employee hiring and scheduling; costume designs (the young ladies at the concession stand all wore flapper style dresses from the 1920s and the gentlemen wore tuxedos) and inventory control and purchasing. Her initial responsibilities involved pretty much everything that had to do with concession sales.

Burruss also helped in programming and with the day-to-day operations of the Byrd, but her biggest contributions came in producing the first two Christmas Celebrations while still at VCU. After VCU, Burruss moved to New York City to pursue a career in fashion merchandising but her involvement with the Byrd didn't end. While in New York, she would take leaves of absence to return to Richmond to produce the 1987 and 1988 Christmas Celebrations.

While planning the 1988 Christmas Celebration, Richards, Snyder and I met with Burruss in New York City to check out some of the shows, gather some ideas, eat well, and to have a good time. One Wednesday night, we took the train into Harlem to attend the Apollo Theater's amateur night.

The first thing we noticed about the historic Apollo Theater is that the theater has as many lights facing the audience as facing the entertainers on the stage. The audience is as much a part of the show as the entertainment. The Apollo has about forty acts in an evening's show. The majority of these acts are singers or singing groups backed by a common band. Some of the acts are magicians, and some are comedians, but the one thing they all have in common is that they all know that this is their big chance to make it in, "Show Business."

If they make it at the Apollo, they can make it anywhere.

And then there's the big hook. If you get the hook, you're back to doing whatever you were doing before, probably for the rest of your life; not too many second chances at the Apollo.

We were into the fourth act when this little girl, who was introduced as being only thirteen years old, took the stage. She wasn't exactly dressed for the Apollo and the microphone was too high on the stand, so you couldn't hear her at first, and of course the audience let her know it. She had trouble getting the musicians on cue, but then again, the audience was booing her so loudly she probably couldn't hear herself think, much less hear the musicians.

Cat calls, boos and balled up paper started flying and just when we thought the hook was coming; that little girl grabbed the microphone, placed it closer to her mouth and started to sing, and oh, what a glorious sound. Within seconds, the audience was dead silent, sitting in almost disbelief. That was absolutely the most incredible sight and sound the Apollo witnessed that night.

For fifteen minutes the audience stood and applauded her in appreciation; and deservedly so. Much of the audience left soon after and none of us could remember her name. Who was she? Lauryn Hill—now a well-known singer, songwriter and rapper.

It wasn't uncommon to see some really cool acts at the Apollo. We would take many trips to New York City to help refuel our creativity. Seeing the kinds of entertainment you can only see on and off-Broadway raised the bar for entertainment at the Byrd Theatre. We at the Byrd would strive to offer exceptional entertainment using as much local talent as possible. The wonderful thing about our

Christmas Celebrations was that we used only local talent.

CHAPTER THIRTEEN
The Impresario

I couldn't sleep at all that night.

Actually, no one in the entire "Company" could sleep that night; no one had slept well for weeks. After all, this was the biggest live show to be produced in the Byrd's history and everyone had the jitters.

There was the huge investment, the huge payroll, the set designs and construction, the costumes, the lights, the sound, the egos. The Byrd's physical stage was readied for such a big show the year before; the only change for this show was to uncover and restore the orchestra pit making room for Doug Richards and his Great American Music Ensemble.

Producing a show on paper is the easy part. Taking that show from the paper to the stage is the tough part. So many pieces must come together to produce a show. And although there were previous shows at the Byrd to help pave the way, every show has its own idiosyncrasies and problems, and this show was so much bigger than anything we'd done before.

Although there were understudies, many of the headliners were so skilled and masterful at their art, there were no understudies available in the world who could substitute for these principals.

The company of the 1988 Christmas Celebration consisted of myself as executive producer, producer Mary Burruss, director John Glenn, conductor Doug Richards, choreographer Melanie Richards, juggler David Hirschi, puppeteer Terry Snyder, harpist Carol Coons, Six Carolers, twelve Byrdettes (in all the shows there were eighteen Byrdettes) sixteen Musicians, several associate producers, sound and lighting engineers and stage hands. And then there was everyone in the front of the house: concessionaires, ushers and house managers. It's tough to fathom the responsibility when everyone's pay, everyone's career, and a theatre's future can sometimes rely on the success of a single show.

I felt good about opening night. The show was smooth. It felt good and the audience showed their appreciation with a twenty minute standing ovation. After the show, most of the cast and company went their separate ways. Some went to clubs, some went to restaurants, but most of them went home and straight to bed; they must have been exhausted.

Rudisill, Barnett, Cowardin and I would always go to Joe's Inn to grab a bite to eat, hang out and ... wait. By 4:30 a.m., a couple of hours after Joe's Inn closed; the morning newspaper and the first review would arrive at the newsstand.

I would often spend those two and a half hours walking the streets of The Fan alone. There were so many things running through my mind: so many scenarios of what to do if the show was poorly reviewed; what to do to make the show better. I was so exhausted, I could barely walk, barely keep my eyes open; what if the reviews were bad?

CHAPTER FOURTEEN
Miracle on Cary Street

The 1988 Christmas Celebration would become the crowning achievement in the Byrd's live theatrical entertainment history. It was the first time a movie wasn't shown in conjunction with a live presentation. By any stretch of the imagination, this was an exceptional show. The reviews were phenomenal! On the front page of the entertainment section, Roy Proctor's review said it all, "Call Byrd's new Christmas show city's own 'Miracle on Cary Street!' This "Christmas Celebration" is a revelation." I couldn't have read better headlines and reviews if I had written them myself.

The success of the 1988 Christmas Celebration would open the door to a lot of new opportunities. First and foremost, this would be the show that lured The Walt Disney Company into the Byrd. This was a big deal with lots of national recognition, fame, and fortune to follow. This would also be the show that after a late night rehearsal, George Stitzer, a previous Byrd manager would make his presence known.

Call Byrd's new Christmas show
city's own 'Miracle on Cary Street'

THEATER REVIEW
By Roy Proctor
News Leader arts editor

When the Byrd Theatre staged its first, "Christmas Celebration" in 1986, that rudimentary front-of-the-curtain show lasted 40 minutes and accompanied the movie "Miracle on 34th Street." Last year's edition grew to an hour on a reclaimed stage, but it still accompanied a movie. This year the movie is gone. Good riddance! You will never miss it.

With the movie-length "Christmas Celebration" that opened last night, this majestic movie palace has come theatrically into its own. The concept, staging, design and technical know-how are light years ahead of previous Byrd revue efforts. Byrd manager Duane Nelson and company have created, in effect, Richmond theater's own "Miracle on Cary Street."

However, the extent to which this is true is not immediately apparent. The four opening numbers are assured, engaging, lively to look at, lovely to hear, but relatively low keyed. They begin with Doug Richards and his Great American Music Ensemble making robust Big Band sounds in the Byrd's reclaimed orchestra pit.

The curtain rises on Ron Keller's magical first-act set, wonderfully lighted by Lou Szari, in which three flights of white stairs are set against a sky blazing with stars and a Christmas tree that seems to float in space. That setting provides all the grand entrances any high-kicking Byrdette could want, but the first Byrdettes number, splendidly costumed by Nancy Allen, is stylishly restrained, at times almost in slow-motion.

Next up is David Hirschi, a veteran Byrd crowd-charmer who scales new heights in an extended act that adds magic to his usual mix of juggling and humor. Then it's the Byrdettes' turn again, this time with an intriguingly oriental-flavored "Chinoiserie" precision dance number.

So much for starters. The incredible warmth that makes this show such a rouser begins in earnest with the introduction of the new Byrd Theatre Choraliers, a vocal sextet that soon proves it can sing anything–and frequently does. James Hughes mans the Mighty Wurlitzer, Carol Coons plucks her celestial instrument in the harp alcove.

The medley that follows is wonderful. Puppeteer Terry Snyder provides the perfect visual accompaniment for "The Skater's Waltz" with a large skating marionette, and Choralier Sean Clerkin turns his lovely tenor to breath-suspending effect on "Silent Night," first in German, then in English.

When that medley leads into an audience sing-along led by the Choraliers, the audience is fully hooked into a warmth that binds it, the performers and the ornate house into a single force. Except for a sound imbalance that permitted the Great American Music Ensemble to drown out the singers occasionally at the top of the second act last night, the enchantment never flags under John Glenn's direction.

Keller's second-act scenery, which turns a farm scene into an interior by means of a turntable and flying scenery, is a wonderful setting for the Choraliers to romp through two medleys of secular Christmas songs, one of which is designed to appeal especially to children.

A Choraliers rendering of "The Twelve Days of Christmas," in which each imaginative costumed Byrdette represents the gift of a different day, is hilariously inventive, and the spiffily costumed "March of the Toy Soldiers" finale, which has become the Byrdettes signature precision number, has never been performed better by Richmond's answer to the Rockettes.

This "Christmas Celebration" is a revelation, Nelson, who produced it, has taken a vestigial stagehouse with seemingly minimal potential -most Richmonders didn't know it existed three years ago-and shown what wonders it can yield in talented hands after three years of inspired tinkering.

By all means, experience it.

"The Byrd Christmas Celebration" a holiday revue at the Byrd Theatre through Dec. 18. Created and produced by Duane K. Nelson, directed by John Glenn, Great American Music Ensemble directed by Doug Richards, Byrdettes choreographed by Melanie Richards; scenery by Ron Keller; lighting by Lou Szari; Byrdette costume designed by Nancy Allen; sound by Gene Fox.

With juggler David Hirschi; puppeteer Terry Snyder; harpist Carol Coons; Debbie Barnes, Reggie Clemon, Sean Clerkin, Jennifer Jones, Michael Joyner, and Debra Wagoner, as Byrd Theatre Choraliers; Rebecca Weiss, Teresa Adams, Deborah Arenstein, Colleen Banister, Dawn Day, Jennefer Fewell, Rita Hinton, Lisa Jackson, Julia Reid, Elizebeth Mathews, Tanya Moring, and Kim Ward as Byrdettes; and Doug Richards, Skip Gales, Greg Luffy, AJ Waters, Breet Young, Fred Kock, Roy Muth, John D'Earth, Mike Davison, Greg Little, Tim Stresgle, Brian Zabrigkis, Dean Englart, Weldon Hill, Clarence Seay and Howard Curtis in the Great American Music Ensemble.

Wonders abound at the Byrd

CRITIC
AT LARGE
By Roy Proctor

"The new West End theater is one of the handsomest in the city, with an interior of great beauty," The News Leader reported one week before the Byrd Theatre opened Christmas Eve 1928. "It is furnished with the most modern equipment, including sound devices and an up-to-date projection room.

"The stage *will be adapted for presentation of plays* as well as motion pictures."

The italics are mine. The reporting was based on the good intentions of the Byrd's original owners. The fulfillment of that original intention, as it turns out, occurred almost 60 years later when, last weekend, the opening of the third annual "Byrd Theatre Christmas Celebration" proved once and for all that the Byrd does indeed have a viable stage.

That's not to say that the stage had not been usable previously. In the two decades before a Cinemascope screen was instead at the front of the Byrd stage and effectively blocked it off, stage shows-mostly musical programs featuring large on-stage orchestras-were offered on rare occasions in conjunction with movies.

In April 1936, for example, radio personality Phil Spitalny and his "Charm Girls," advertised as "30 sirens of syncopation," held fourth in a 60-minute show four times a day for a week.

However, from the day it opened, the Byrd's ability to "be adapted for presentation of plays as well as motion pictures" was severely limited by historical events.

"The Jazz Singer," which opened here in January 1928

at the Capitol Theatre, launched the mushrooming demand for cheap "talkies." The Depression, just around the corner, made cheapness a prime consideration for Richmond's entertainment-seeking masses. The theatrical "road" died, and, for all practical purposes, the Byrd's theatrical utility died with it.

The magical transformation of the Byrd into a legitimate theater for this "Christmas Celebration" is nothing short of astonishing. The scenery, costumes, lighting and sound are highly professional. The show flows in the best sense. The stage offers two complete changes of scenery, and they're accomplished by flying scenic elements, a turntable and other staging niceties.

This didn't happen all at once, of course. When the Byrd recruited Randy Strawderman to form the Byrdettes as the centerpiece of its first 40-minute "Christmas Celebration" in 1986, that wide screen was still firmly in place.

All the performers had to enter the stage-only a "lip" in front of the gold Austrian curtains-from the auditorium. Most of the music was recorded. The lighting was little more than flood-lighting. The floor was so rough that the tap-dancing sounds of the Byrdettes had to be prerecorded.

Yet there was something magical about that first "Christmas Celebration." The transformation for last Christmas' 60-minute version was spectacular. Byrd manager Duane Nelson had figured out a way to "fly" the movie screen out of sight.

That revealed the Byrd's stage for the first time since the 1950s and yielded a total stage depth of 22 feet-including the lip that had been built over that had originally been an orchestral pit-on both sides of the proscenium arch. (By comparison, the stage depth, not counting the orchestral pits, is 46 feet at the Carpenter Center and 33 feet at the Empire Theatre).

Scenic pizazz was now possible, and top Richmond

designer Ron Keller met the challenge with a set that centered on a magical fireplace and was largely filled with a handsome bandstand for the second "Christmas Celebration."

Trouble was, such a massive onstage bandstand took up too much room. The solution was obvious: Uncover and restore the original orchestra pit to house the Great American Music Ensemble while rigging the fly space to facilitate scenic changes and effects.

This fall, Richmond movie-palace lover Miles Rudisill and associates donated their time and carpentry skills to restore the pit, according to Nelson.

Work on rigging the fly space continued apace (only half the available space is rigged for this show). A Permanent Masonite stage floor was installed. A top-of the-line wireless sound system was rented from Herndon's Wireless Systems Inc. which is providing the sound system for Broadway's "Phantom of the Opera."

All of this made the visual and aural splendor now arrayed at the Byrd possible on a total production budget of $81,000, every penny of which can be clearly seen and heard in the show now running.

Uncovering the orchestra pit involved a sacrifice of sorts. It reduced the distance from the front of the stage to the back wall to 15 feet. Given the ingenuity already expended, don't be surprised if Nelson and company figure out a way to reclaim the lost seven feet for shows that do not require the pit.

Even if they don't, what's possible on a stage 37 feet wide and 15 feet deep with an orchestra pit, fly capability and some wing space? Much more magic than you might believe possible.

Most road musicals won't fit on a stage this size, although intimate traveling revues might well do so. The backstage amenities- the Byrdettes, for example, are dressing in two trailers parked across an alley behind the Byrd-may not meet Equity standards.

However, most plays and almost any kind of show specifically designed for the Byrd would fit on its stage handily. With the run of "Christmas Celebration" only half over, Nelson, Keller and company are already dreaming of more and better shows to come-and no wonder!

Indeed, the Byrd involves many wonders. It's a wonder it's always been preserved as well as it has. It's a wonder it continues to function as a movie house-and profitable, Nelson says-in an age when most other vintage American movie palaces have either been razed, abandoned or, as in the case of the Carpenter Center, converted to other uses.

The Byrd's present staging achievement and continued potential are, simply put, incomparable resources for Richmond theater.

Roy Proctor is The News Leader's arts editor.

THE PICTURE
THE PICTUR

**Richmond's Historic
Byrd Theatre**

CHAPTER FIFTEEN
George Stitzer

One big difference between the 1987 and 1988 Christmas Celebrations is that the 1987 show didn't have a stage to rehearse on; all rehearsals were performed outside the Byrd on makeshift; temporary stages. And although the Byrd never preempted a scheduled show or movie for a rehearsal, the 1988 stage was almost always available for rehearsals after midnight and most mornings. Since most of the Byrdettes had full time jobs or school, the best time for Byrdette rehearsals would be on Saturday and Sunday mornings.

One Sunday morning, I arrived early to see how the show was coming along. Most of the company wouldn't arrive for another hour so I wasn't surprised that no one was there to greet me, but I was a little alarmed that the front door was unlocked and most of the cleaning lights were still on.

That meant John Archie, the janitor, was still there. I knew Archie, who was also a Baptist preacher, should have been at his church by then. I called out for Archie, but to no avail, and still having an hour before rehearsal, went over to the church to check on Archie.

He told me a story that would stay with me for the rest of my life. Archie was cleaning near the stage area, listening to some church music from an old boom box the Byrdettes used. He was on the far side of the stage when the boom box just stopped playing. Archie headed over to the boom box side of the stage to turn the music back on. Then he returned to the other side of the stage to resume cleaning.

The music stopped again.

Archie headed back over to the boombox, but this time he was met by a man—a strange looking man he had never seen before.

I can vouch for the fact that The Byrd is a little spooky late at night. The lights are dim, the building makes all kinds of strange sounds and everything seems a little foggy.

Archie gave a pretty good description of the stranger. He described the man as average height and weight, dark hair, mid-fifties in age, and wearing a tuxedo. The man seemed a little perturbed, had his arms crossed, was tapping his foot and constantly clearing his throat.

"The man looked upset ... very upset!"

Archie didn't want to stick around to find out why. He ran out of the theatre and kept running, another half mile to his church.

That morning when I spoke to Archie at church, I could see he was still a little upset. I had to laugh when he apologized for not locking the front door.

For the next couple of days, everyone associated with the Byrd tried to think of who that man could have been. It wasn't until the Christmas Celebration's opening night that we found out who he was.

Just before the Byrd opened her doors for the 1988 Christmas Celebration; Miles Rudisill "held court" in the lobby. With him was a large scrapbook of the theatre going back to the 1950s when he first became associated with the place.

Everyone who wasn't getting ready for the show was there. The lobby was packed and as Rudisill thumbed through the pages revealing decades of history and generations of memories, John Archie yelled out, "That's him ... that's the man I saw!"

On a full page in the middle of the scrap book was a picture of George Stitzer, a man in his late fifties, arms crossed and wearing a tuxedo. Stitzer was associated with the Byrd Theatre for nearly fifty years. He was the assistant manager under Robert Coulter and then the manager of the Byrd until 1979.

He was remembered for constantly tapping his foot, clearing his throat, and always being upset about something.

He was murdered just a few blocks from the theatre in 1979 while making a bank deposit. I don't think anyone, from that day on, went into the Byrd theatre alone. The Byrd was haunted!

CHAPTER SIXTEEN
Walt Disney Company

About the same time, during one of the Christmas Celebration's rehearsals, Rod Rodriguez, a top Disney executive visited the Byrd. He was so impressed with the rehearsals that on opening night he came back to see the show live, but with him this time was Michael Eisner, CEO of Disney.

In 1988, the two main exhibitors in Richmond were Cineplex Odeon and United Artists. Cineplex Odeon had just purchased Neighborhood Theatres and controlled half of the film exhibitions in Richmond; United Artist controlled the other half.

What happened in January 1989 was incredible luck for the Byrd Theatre. Cineplex Odeon and United Artists entered into a film exhibition war with Disney and boycotted Disney. For an entire year, the only two first run exhibitors in Richmond, Virginia refused to play Disney films. And the only independent theatre in town was now the beautiful Byrd Theatre.

In January of 1989, the Byrd Theatre started doing what it hadn't done since the Hollywood Antitrust Act of 1948 and began exhibiting Disney films exclusively. For the first six months Disney exhibited such films as *Oliver And Company, Dead Poets Society, and Honey, I Shrunk the Kids.* As in the 1930s and 1940s, the Byrd Theatre would schedule shows all day, often bringing in new features weekly to accommodate huge crowds. For the first six months in 1989, the Byrd Theatre needed every single one of the thirteen hundred plus seats. The Byrd Theatre was on a roll.

Unfortunately, Cable's restaurant in Tampa, Florida was not doing so well and by the middle of 1989, Cable and the Warrens were at war.

The investment in Tampa far exceeded the Warren's investment at the Byrd and as I said many times, it would be that restaurant that would determine the future of the Byrd Theatre.

Blame for the Tampa problem was thrown in all directions. There were probably cost overruns on the development and construction of the restaurant and there were probably trumped up market feasibility studies illustrating the need for such a fine dining establishment in Tampa. Although I had only seen pictures, it was one of the most beautiful restaurants I'd ever seen.

In the way of furnishings, the restaurant was full of antiques, brass railings, crystal chandeliers, and even exotic worm-eaten walnut paneling. The restaurant had all of the characteristics and charm of the Tobacco Company in Richmond.

Cable had a firm hand in management controls. He had two good managers in Jack McNamee and Jack McGrath, and so I felt certain the operation's loss problem lay elsewhere.

Tampa, Florida had the wealth and population to support a large fine dining restaurant, but did it want to? Especially one across the street from Busch Gardens on Busch Boulevard? Regardless of the problems in Tampa, I was caught in the crossfire. So, from June to December, 1989, I was out of the Byrd Theatre.

This caused some problems with the Byrd.

All of the exhibition rights were in my name. When Cineplex Odeon and United Artist made a truce, instead of showing films exclusively, the Byrd started splitting screens on exhibition with two other theatres in Richmond. If I had been there, Disney would have had to exhibit exclusively with the Byrd for the remainder of the year.

Unfortunately, this affected the attendance and the dollars earned on concessions. Attendance declined from an average of twelve thousand patrons a week down to an average of three thousand patrons a week. By the end of 1989, Disney was out of the Byrd, Cable was out of the Byrd and the Byrd Theatre was again closed!

CHAPTER SEVENTEEN
Intermission

Five years of my life had been consumed with the idea of making a success of the Byrd Theatre. I spent most nights in the building making sure the operations were sound and the presentations were as I wished. And most importantly, I wanted to ensure what little money the Byrd made, actually made it to the bank.

The one thing I had always been told about the restaurant business, and the Byrd's concessions makes it a restaurant business, is that what isn't stolen and taken out of the front door will certainly be stolen and taken out of the back door.

Not to say theft is inherent in the restaurant business and every employee is a potential crook, but when one is tempted with money in an all cash environment, morals are bent and often bent with creativity.

As an example, everyone in the theatre business knows the biggest profit margins are in the concessions and inventory controls of these concessions are an absolute must. We don't inventory popcorn kernels; we do inventory popcorn containers.

Popcorn containers arrive in cases and each popcorn container represents a dollar amount, so when you start with a hundred containers and you sell five containers at $3.00 a pop; you should have $15.00 extra in the till and ninety-five popcorn containers still in your inventory. So, this is how an otherwise sweet concessionaire found her way into confiscating, about $200 over the course of several weeks.

The Byrd Theatre was always clean and presentable to our patrons. To accomplish this, the entire staff would clean the theatre between shows. This was one reason why there were always so many long lines formed outside the theatre for the 9:45 shows and midnight shows on weekends.

When I say the entire staff, I mean the entire staff. The projectionist, Brenograph and spotlight operators would hit the balcony first and then would help out the concessionaires and management with the main auditorium.

The Byrd was a mess after the 7:15 shows and the 9:45 shows on weekends. Popcorn, butter and soda were everywhere. The seats didn't have the springs necessary for lifting the seat bottoms back to the upright position, so they all had to be lifted by hand. The drink and popcorn containers all had to be picked up and the entire place had to be swept, vacuumed and mopped clean. Only then would we allow patrons to enter the building; always keeping in mind our motto, "We sell tickets to theatres, not movies."

Someway, somehow, the used popcorn containers instead of finding their way into the garbage containers where they belonged, would find their way to the bottom of the inventory and thus be accounted for as unsold. The good thing is that those used containers were never resold and would be discarded as damaged inventory. The bad thing? I had to terminate the employment of one of the nicest concessionaires who ever worked for me.

And that's only one reason why it was a good idea for me to be at the theatre every night.

All of the other theatre business such as film bookings, purchasing, and paying the bills had to be performed during the day; Monday through Friday. And since I couldn't afford a secretary, I spent most of my time hanging out by the phone waiting for phone calls. Remember, this was 1989 and not many people were using cell phones yet.

I hung out in the office for hours at a time waiting on important phone calls and getting that last film booking necessary to complete a scheduling deadline.

During my six months away from the Byrd, I had the time to think about some things and do some things I didn't have time to do before. One of those things was sailing.

I remember answering an ad in the *Richmond Times Dispatch* that read: "Sailing and Seamanship; Weekend course; Three days, two nights on the beautiful Rappahannock River." I thought, "What a better way for the unemployed to spend a weekend than on the beautiful Rappahannock River sailing."

I signed up and on Friday morning I set off from Richmond and drove through some of the most beautiful countryside in Virginia to a sleepy little town called Urbanna. There, I boarded a 32-foot yacht named *Dorothy* and with two couples (talk about being the fifth wheel) ventured down one of the most beautiful rivers in North America to the Chesapeake Bay.

I felt like an adventurer, an explorer, maybe what Captain John Smith may have felt like when entering the Americas for the first time in the early 17th century. It was raining most of the weekend and it was colder than it should have been. I was feeling rather seasick most of the time, but I knew from that moment, that sailing and adventure would be my destiny.

It's funny, but when I left the Byrd for unemployment, my only thoughts were of despair, but in hindsight, I can only thank the war between the Warrens and Cable for introducing me to such a wonderful and enlightening experience. And although I didn't know it at the time, sailing would become my life's pursuit—a purpose.

There were some other interests I picked up in the 1990s. One would be golf.

Golf would take me away from the Byrd on Saturday mornings to the beautiful fairways of some of Virginia's finest courses. I wish I could say that with some sincerity. The only fairways I got to see were those closest to the woods from where I was normally playing. My drives off the tees produced some of the biggest slices possible and if it wasn't for the ball hitting the trees along the edges of the fairways and ricocheting back on to the fairways, I would be playing most of my second shots from the woods.

And, although some of the fellows I "teed off" with quite often played on those illustrious fairways, it was the fellowship enjoyed throughout the round of golf, on the tees and greens, that made golfing on those Saturday morning all worthwhile.

Manfred Duggins was our golf ring leader. He was a great golfer. He didn't rank in the world, didn't hold any records, never played in a PGA tournament and he seldom played with anyone except his friends, but he was a great golfer.

Actually, I think he did hold one record; more likely to be found in *Ripley's Believe It or Not* than the *Guinness Book*.

When Manfred Duggins traded in his old car for a new one, the story goes that it took him three and a half hours just to move all of the golf paraphernalia from the old car trunk to the new car trunk. In this collection of golf paraphernalia were fifteen 5 woods, seven 13 woods, a couple 11 woods, eight drivers, a collection of short and long putters, six sand wedges and a custom-made 19 wood, not to mention a thousand golf balls (ladies high compression) and ten thousand tees (not only scattered throughout the trunk and the rest of the car, but usually found in the house, the office, Buddy's Place, etc..). In addition, along with the rest of the golf clubs in his bag, he always carried a supply of "aiming juice" (aka Scotch whiskey.)

With a name like Duggins, you best believe the aiming juice is going to be from Ireland, not Scotland; SCOTLAND! I meant SCOTLAND, not Ireland! Sorry Manfred.

So every Saturday from the mid 1990s to the mid 2000s, all of my golfing friends and I would meet on some golf course (somewhere) around six in the morning to enjoy a beautiful day of golf or a walk in the woods. I am pretty sure that I met every single one of these guys through Manfred Duggins.

Some of the guys I played with were Bill (Cabo) Cabaniss, Jimmy (Bobo) Mitchell, Brad Smallwood, Richard (Huggie) Longmire, James Earl Dudley, Bookie Boland, Charlie Diradour and from the Charlottesville, Virginia, area, Thomas (Zipper) Lippmann, Paul Lippmann, Joe Graham, Andy Manning and David Elkins (Actually, I met David Elkins sailing in Urbanna).

In those six months away from the Byrd, I made some promises to myself. I made a promise that I would make the Byrd Theatre so popular and viable that it would be impossible for anyone to tear her down and I promised I would reach the financial goals that would allow me to continue my sailing journeys of exploration.

I wanted to see this entire wonderful world. I had a ten year plan, but it took seventeen, and it was a yo-yo of an experience.

CHAPTER EIGHTEEN
A New Beginning and a New Hope

In December of 1989, Rudisill and I traveled to Arlington, Virginia, to meet with Samuel and Irma Warren, the owners of the Byrd Theatre.

At this time, I was led to believe the Warrens were worth well over $100 million. I was surprised that the meeting was to take place at the Warren's home, rather than a hotel in Fredericksburg where meetings usually took place. I was even more surprised at the condition of the Warrens' home.

Their once-beautiful colonial style house showed significant signs of deterioration and lack of maintenance. The wrought iron fence surrounding the property was rusty and damaged from fallen trees. There was an old pickup truck on cinder blocks in the driveway, again rusty and probably not driven in decades.

I figured we must have gotten the wrong address. This house was certainly abandoned and on the verge of falling down. But it was the right house and shortly after knocking, the front door was answered by none other than Samuel Warren.

Mr. Warren welcomed us in with a smile and introduced us to one of his children. Mrs. Warren, who wasn't well, came downstairs to welcome us. Mrs. Warren then kindly made her excuses and proceeded back upstairs.

I'd met with the Warrens several times over the past seven years. Since the previous time, Mrs. Warren had lost a lot of weight and looked ill. I didn't know it then, but that would be the last time I would see Mrs. Warren alive.

The interior of the Warrens' home was even more dilapidated than the exterior. In the living room, wallpaper was peeling from the walls; the once plush wall-to-wall carpet had traffic patterns throughout the house and was so worn down you could see the underlying hardwood floors. The dining room had a 1950s Formica table, probably from some fast food restaurant they owned. All of the chairs were mismatched, again looking as if they were from various restaurants the Warrens may have owned at some time.

Next to the dining room was a sunroom. The room was so filled with file boxes, there wasn't even a path to walk through. The room certainly hadn't been used in some time.

The kitchen was dated and the sink drain didn't work so a bucket placed beneath the sink had to be emptied every so often. This was done by opening the back door and throwing the waste water on the back lawn. With all things considered, the Warrens appeared more in rags than in riches and most certainly seemed not to be the millionaires I thought they were.

But appearances lacking, the Warrens were every bit as wealthy as believed. The Warrens owned large parcels of property in and around Arlington, Virginia. They may not have owned the property where Dulles Airport was built, but they often spoke of a farm they owned at one time in the near vicinity.

Hopefully, their properties didn't all look like their home, even though they probably did (the properties we know about certainly did).

I found the Warrens eccentric. When it came to the property they owned, they seemed to care more about the quantity than the quality.

This made me nervous for several reasons. The Byrd was in need of some immediate structural repairs and from the looks of things, the Warrens were not going to supply the funds to make those repairs.

The Byrd-type of theater was obsolete and would continue to be so. Could the Warrens be made to understand this? I didn't think so. I could have gotten a better response if talking to a wall when speaking about foundations, tax credits, 501(c)(3) foundations and non-profit organizations. The Byrd had to be appreciated as an educational and entertainment center within the Richmond, Virginia, community and wouldn't be saved unless she was open and being enjoyed!

A contract was drawn and I signed a year-to-year lease on the Byrd Theatre. Without Disney and with the Byrd currently closed, a lot of liability was shifted to my corner. The triple net agreement stipulated that I would pay the Warrens $5,000 a month and pay all of the operating expenses. The Warrens would pay the real estate taxes and the cost for a new roof.

The new roof never materialized.

Just about everything promised by the Warrens never materialized and because of this and past experiences with the Warrens, I never felt optimistic about the Byrd Theatre's future. The rough years were passing and now Carytown was on an upswing and was no longer considered a "dangerous" area of town. The parking situation was better with the building of a new public parking deck behind the Byrd. There were still many problems with Carytown, but they were manageable.

The real problem was what to do with the Byrd? What new concept could be dreamed up to bring in growing audiences?

The Byrd also looked worn; after all, I had been away from the Byrd for six months. Money had to be spent on new carpet, furnishings, roof repair, seat repair, utility deposits, film guarantees, payroll, operating capital, and much more. If the Byrd was to be saved, it was imperative that the Byrd maintained the appearance of a successful operation.

The first meeting I had as the sole proprietor of the Byrd Theatre's operating company was with Sam Bendheim, who had just bought back the Neighborhood Theatre chain his father and Morton Thalhimer's father had founded at the turn of the nineteenth century. It was great having lunch with my old boss. The next meeting was with my friends, Rudisill, Cowardin, and Barnett.

The new concept I introduced to them didn't go over well at first. It involved lowering prices, showing current films newly released from first run, doing away with the printed schedule and relying on daily display ads that could be modified quickly and inexpensively.

With this new format, the Byrd would be locked in only for weekly runs, and could still show double bills, but with the flexibility of changing show times and features on a weekly basis.

If a film laid an egg, the theatre would have to suffer through it for only one week.

CHAPTER NINETEEN
Open Again

Next on the agenda was to actually open the Byrd to the public, which was accomplished by the end of January 1990. This new concept wasn't an overnight success, but by that summer, we started to see some light again.

The Byrd found her niche in exhibiting newly released first run films on a discount second run basis. By the end of the summer, she was averaging around three thousand patrons a week. Next up was making the Byrd Theatre beautiful again!

In 1990, the theatre had three different carpet patterns in three different areas of the theatre. The newest was a plush high pile carpet laid in 1984 and covered the down stairs, lobby and foyer. In only six years, this carpet was starting to show some wear, tear and traffic patterns.

There was still some of the 1928 wool carpet on the mezzanine and some of the 1940 wool carpet still in the balcony. Although both of these carpets appeared in fine shape, they were dry rotted and their seams were difficult to repair, making it hazardous in the low movie house lighting conditions at the Byrd. And, since we wanted to open the balcony we had to remedy this situation.

The first thing was to remove the old carpets, have them cleaned, bound into throw rugs, and stored to serve as rug patterns for future replication. These rugs were loaned to Maynee Cayton of Bygones Vintage Clothing next to the Byrd Theatre. She was always accommodating in costuming the Byrd's Concessionaires and ushers, and in her care we knew the carpets would be safely displayed.

Next up was to install a durable carpet that could stand up to just about anything. A red, low-pile carpet was located and installed, and replaced in part every three years from 1990 to 2004. The original carpet would cost around $200 a square yard to reproduce; we purchased this carpet for $21 a square yard, installed. New carpet cost with installation would average around $20,000 initially and then about a third of that for maintenance and partial replacement every three years.

All of the antique furniture in use at the Byrd between 1984 and 1989 belonged to Jerry Cable; when he left, so did the antiques. I purchased and replaced all of them in 1990.

The next stop was with Gary Thomas and Governors Antiques where I bought most of the mirrors and other furnishings. Rudisill was most helpful in this endeavor. The large portrait mirrors, floor and ceiling lamps, and chairs were of the 1890, antebellum, Italian baroque, and French Renaissance design.

Our thinking was anything placed in the Byrd should be of late 1920s vintage or earlier, sturdy enough to take the everyday beating of normal theatre operations, but elegant enough to complement the Byrd's architectural style. Rudisill would refer to the interior design as "very movie mojo." This also goes along with the concept that the show begins as soon as one enters the theatre, unlike today's cinemas where the show exists only on the screen.

As "Roxy" famously said, "We sell tickets to theaters, not movies." I envisioned that same philosophy underlying everything at the Byrd; the show begins as soon as you walk through the front doors.

The 1940 neon marquee at the Byrd was once a beautiful sight, visible for many blocks on Cary Street. But during the 1960s, probably when the roof was replaced, it was replaced with a new modern looking marquee. There were many thoughts as to why this was done, most agreed the original marquee leaked, which cost a lot to maintain and keep in good repair. Just changing all of the light bulbs must have been both expensive and an incredibly troublesome task.

I don't know how they managed to re-lamp the vertical Byrd sign; they either hired a crane or a mountain climber. Re-lamping is a high operating expense inherited at the Byrd with tens of thousands of light bulbs in the interior that require frequent cleaning and replacement. There are a great many brass doors and fixtures that also need continuous polishing, maintenance, and repair.

Keeping the seats in a usable condition was also costly. Not only did seat springs shoot out here or there, but often the pot metal frames would break and the forged metal would bend. Sometimes the forged metal could be reshaped, but most often the cast parts couldn't be welded or repaired and had to be re-fabricated at an enormous expense.

Rudisill would often sew new fabric into the seats for only the cost of the fabric, but welders and metal smiths were like bank robbers with a never ending supply of banks to rob. After reassembly, Rudisill, Archie, and I would re-install them after midnight.

And although the brass, the crystal, and the marble garner immediate attention, take a closer look at the foundation and structural fabric of the theatre. Here is where the Byrd is made of concrete and steel. Even the lathe that supports the plaster is metal, not wood, and accounts for how the Byrd has maintained her integrity for all of these years and how she can be affordably restored.

Most cinemas of today are built like movie sets that would last only twenty or so years. The Byrd was built like a palace for generations to enjoy!

The Mighty Wurlitzer

SPECIAL ENGAGEMENT
AN EXTRAORDINARY
EVENT

WINGS

1927

BYRD
SINCE 1928

ADMIT ONE
ANY REGULAR

ADMIT ONE:
ANY REGULAR

ADMIT ONE
ANY REGULAR

ADMIT ONE
VIP
PASS
ANY REGULAR
OR SPECIAL

Fanfare, Pl...

For 67 years, the Byrd Th...
most resplendent. Even now, wor...
elegance lacking at the multi-plexes. The ...
digital audio tape; the Byrd is Mozart on a ...

The theater's uniqueness is not ...
Organ rises from below floor level and L...
rises from below floor level and the Wur...
ganist, belts out the Wur...
big-wind sounds — and it's almost...
Weaver all over again. It's a little ...
like the flapper-girl costumes worn by ...
the concessionaires — but then the camp is ...
half the fun.

The other half is listening to a live ...
performance with an instrument few today ...
ever get to hear. Now, Richmonders who ...
enjoy listening to the Wurlitzer when they go out can enjoy it when they stay ...
The Virginia Theater Organ Society and the Byrd have conspired to rele...
Byrd Sings," a compact disc of recordings made with the Wurlitzer ...
Ron Rhode plays the instrument for the recording: Chuck Rhode ...
vocals. The scores range from the Cavalleria Rusticana intermezzo in "Go L...
Over a Four-Leaf Clover." The CD is available at local music stores. Th...
itself, of course, remains on Cary Street ...
fortune, it will stay open for a long ti...

THE PIC...
THE PICTURE...
Richmond's Historic
Byrd Theatre

CHAPTER TWENTY
Art Afternoons at the Byrd

The Byrd was rolling with discount second-run movies at night and on most weekends, attracting long lines wrapped around the building. During the week, particularly on Mondays and Tuesdays, and weekend matinees, attendance was weak. In comes Mike Jones.

I met Mike Jones a couple of years earlier while he was still operating the now defunct Biograph Cinema. Under Terry Rea, the first manager, the Biograph was a fairly successful mainstream art and repertory house for close to twenty years. But because of changes in the cinema viewing audiences, changes in the neighborhood, and many of the same circumstances that had closed other cinemas in Richmond, the Biograph was closed soon after Jones took the helm. This was through no fault of Jones's management or programming style; there just wasn't enough business to support art and independently produced films on a full-time basis. But could the public support them in a series scheduled on weekend afternoons? Again, a plan was discussed, and a prospectus drawn up.

I referred to Jones as "Dr. Jone-*stein.*" This came from the combination of the Indiana Jones films and the Young Frankenstein film and also because Jones was a professor of film, filmmaking, and film history at Virginia Commonwealth University. Jones called me "Nel-*sonabitch*" and no explanation is necessary as to where that came from.

But let it be known that everyone will tell you that "Nel-*sonofabitch*" was one of the nicest, most respected gentlemen in the whole wide world. Helen Marie Taylor once told me that only a war's victors write history books. Perhaps that's because it helps to be *alive* when writing history books; hence, the writing of this book. But, with nicknames and professionalism aside, the two of us set out to bring some good art and independently produced films to the Byrd Theatre on Saturday and Sunday afternoons.

To generate the interest of film buffs, all of the films needed to be reviewed by the critics prior to their showings on weekend matinees. Management provided a 10-week printed schedule describing all of the films, but the critic's reviews were imperative, primarily for the publicity they provided. Most films had no national advertising, therefore the only means of exposure was by paid newspaper ads, house-made flyers, and newspaper critic reviews.

In order to be reviewed, a film had to be first run or new to the Richmond market and have some sort of community appeal that would be deserving of a review. Quite often, an interview with the film's stars would follow a critic's screening. The prints were shipped early every Thursday morning. Newspaper critic Carole Kass, Jones, and I would sit through (and sometimes painfully endure) the many art and independent films we would bring to Richmond film lovers.

Most of these films were wonderful, but occasionally, a dud would appear. Even if she walked out of a screening looking bewildered, Kass could always be relied on to provide a good review on Friday morning. Most of the films were good; *The Vanishing*, although released in 1990, played at the Byrd, first run, in 1991.

Also included in the "Art Afternoons" programming were the 19th and 20th International Tournée of Animation, popular amongst filmmakers and enthusiasts from countries all around the world.

Many of the first works by Pixar were included in these presentations.

All in all, "Art Afternoons at the Byrd" were successful, but that success was short lived. Within two years, the Westhampton Theater would begin showing similar programming, but guaranteeing longer runs and evening shows. Even though Mike Jones's art programming was short lived, his many other connections in the film industry and with VCU helped the Byrd for many years to come.

Jones introduced four important Richmond citizens to me in the early 1990s. The first were Drs. Peter and Francoise Kirkpatrick, professors of French literature, culture and film studies at Virginia Commonwealth University and the University of Richmond respectively; and Drs. David and Catherine White, also associated with Virginia Commonwealth University and the Medical College of Virginia.

Drs. Peter & Françoise Kirkpatrick, professors at Virginia Commonwealth University and the University of Richmond, respectively, introduced the city to the French Film Festival, first at Jones' Biograph in 1993 and then at the Byrd in 1996, where it has been a permanent fixture in Richmond ever since. The Festival at the Byrd in 1996 started with a mere few thousand attendees but immediately started by bringing in person the filmmakers and actors to present their films, rather than through teleconferencing. Since 2001, this highly awaited French cultural event now draws annually over twenty thousand attendees.

This is a brilliant vision and flawlessly executed by the Kirkpatricks. What a huge feather in the Byrd's entertainment repertoire! What started out as a couple of movies each night soon became a four day intensive extravaganza spotlighting some of France's newest and boldest cinematic creations presented by a high-profile delegation of filmmakers.

"The Festival has earned acclaim in the U.S. and in France for introducing more than 800 French and francophone films to American audiences. We have welcomed to Richmond over 950 directors, screenwriters, actors, cinematographers, music composers and artists-technicians. Since 2003, it has been acclaimed by French Ambassadors to the U.S. and by prestigious institutions such as the profession's French Writers, Actors, Directors, Musicians, and Artist-Technicians Guilds as the most important French Film Festival outside of France. Those distinctions and the honor of having so many Americans of all ages come to Richmond from across the US to discover French cinema in a spectacular movie palace are all quite humbling. We are so lucky to have a magical venue like the Byrd Theatre in order to pull off every year something of this magnitude," shared the Kirkpatricks.

Other than Cable and me, Drs. David and Catherine White were the only source of financial assistance provided to the Byrd. The Whites were big contributors to Richmond's performing and fine arts community. In the early 1990s, the Byrd was not organized as a non-profit entity, therefore contributions had to be investment oriented with no Federal tax advantage potential. There weren't many investors, if any, available to single-screen movie palaces. While at one time there were thousands of single-screen theaters in the country, by now only a few still existed and the Byrd may have been the only one in the country still open.

The White's requirement was that the loans needed to be attached to me personally and that there would be a "key man" life insurance policy taken out on me for the duration of the loans. Finding outside investors for the theatre would always be a problem, especially considering the owners of the property never invested in their own property beyond the original purchase price.

The Whites were angels to the Byrd Theatre. Besides being a huge help financially to Nelson Communications Company in operating the Byrd, they were also contributors to the Colonel Read Foundation for Courage in the Arts, specifically for the Nelson/ Strawderman musical production, *The Red Badge of Courage* and the Byrd Theatre Foundation many years later.

By the mid-1990s the Byrd started to enjoy a large part of the movie going market audience in Richmond. It never looked better! For the most part, Rudisill kept the place in good cosmetic repair, Cowardin kept the visual and sound equipment in good repair, Barnett kept the mechanical systems running, Barnett and the Virginia Theatre Organ Society kept the organ in good repair, and Opra Archie had joined her husband John in keeping the Byrd clean.

Ever since the George Stitzer sighting, I don't think John Archie ever entered the theatre alone again. But, the theatre's continual increase in business caused cleaning to be a major endeavor, sometimes taking all night. So, Opra and occasionally their children and grandchildren were a welcome help to John; I couldn't blame the ghost of George Stitzer for the added payroll.

As mentioned before, John Archie was a Baptist minister and a good one as I can attest. Every early Sunday morning I could sneak up to the balcony and hear the makings of a sermon playing out down below in the orchestra section. Of course Opra, children and grandchildren were the congregation and all were in the choir as well. So, for every bolt of lightning and brimstone John served up, it was immediately answered by Opra and children with, "Praise the Lord Brother John and Hallelujah!"

And that was just the practice round; the real deal that came later on in the morning was spectacular. I don't know who put the fire under Pastor John Archie, but whoever it was made the fire exceptionally hot. Maybe, George Stitzer had something to do with it.

SPECIAL ENGAGEMENT
AN EXTRAORDINARY
EVENT

WINGS

...tured one of the best war films...
...This epic of World War I stars...
...Charles "Buddy" Rogers, Richard...
...and Gary Cooper. It was the by...
...war films, and will be acc...
...Theatre pipe organ playing...
... musical s...

The Mighty
Wurlitzer

Richmond

TUESDAY

Fanfare, Pleas

For 57 years, the Byrd Th...
...most resplendent. Even now, wor...
...elegance lacking at the multi-plexes...
...digital audio tape; the Byrd is Mozart...

The theater's uniqueness is not b...
Organ the best part of the evening is the m...
...organ rises from below floor level and D...
...parade, house organist, belts out the Wur...
...letters, big-wind sounds — and it's almost...
...Eddie Weaver all over again. It's a little...
...beauty, like the flapper-girl costumes worn by...
...the concessionaires — but then the camp is...
...half the fun.

The other half is listening to a live
...performance with an instrument few today
...ever get to hear. Now, Richmonders who
...enjoy listening to the Wurlitzer when they go out
The Virginia Theater Organ Society and the Byrd have conspired to release...
Byrd Sings," a compact disc of recordings made with the Wurlitzer...
...Ron Rhode plays the instrument for the recording; Chuck Rhode plays...
vocals. The scores range from the Cavalleria Rusticana intermezzo to "I'm Look...
Over a Four-Leaf Clover." The CD is available at local music stores that...
...itself, of course, remains on Cary Street — which, with any luck, it...
...fortune, it will stay open for a long time...

THE PI
THE PICTUR
**Richmond's Historic
Byrd Theatre**

CHAPTER TWENTY-ONE
Making Ends Meet

Although the Byrd was seeing increases in attendance and increases in gross receipts, expenses were on the rise as well, keeping the operation on constant edge. The margins were so narrow that breaking even was a constant struggle.

Every expense in movie exhibitions or live shows is based on a percentage. The box office payout was a percentage of the box office receipts, and although overhead expenses, concession costs, and payroll expenses were fixed, they would still be controlled by a cost percentage of gross revenues. Since no one had control over the amount of business the Byrd would experience, inventory cost controls were the best means of managing income. The only way to increase revenue without raising ticket prices was to bring in additional income from outside of the exhibition business.

This was achieved in several areas by the mid 1990s. First was the introduction of Byrd Dollars.

Byrd Dollars were coupons that could be redeemed at the box office and they all had expiration dates which were strictly enforced. Byrd Dollars were introduced after Thanksgiving Day and sold through the beginning of the next year. They made great stocking stuffers and were advertised as such. The original Byrd dollar was a Disney Dollar-type currency that incorporated a clever design of the Mighty Wurlitzer and was printed on glossy paper stock that was impossible to reproduce.

It was also important not to exceed a certain printing cost; after all, you didn't want your printing costs to exceed your fair value minus your box office costs. By selling packages of ten Byrd Dollars for $7.50, the Byrd could recover $5.00 when redeemed. That was providing film rentals stayed at 35% of the box office receipts.

The key to increasing profits was to rely on a certain percentage of the Byrd Dollars not to be redeemed by the expiration date, which would drive up the profits at the box office. Byrd Dollar packages released during Christmas generated an additional $50,000 at the box office up front. So between the Christmas Celebrations and the Byrd Dollar packages, the Byrd would weather the traditionally slow sales period in December.

With the theatre selling out most shows on Saturday nights and with the balcony stowaways (folks sneaking into the balcony when the balcony is closed) on the rampage; we came up with an idea of selling balcony seating, but at a premium price. So, to be "Above the Rest" would cost a mere dollar extra. Not only would this allow access to the balcony, but also to the mezzanine and exclusive restrooms and parlors separated from the masses down below. An usher, dressed in a tuxedo, would allow you upstairs if and only if you had the right color and priced ticket.

This increased the box office take on Saturday nights. But, as the popularity of the Byrd became more apparent and the attendance was ever-increasing, we had to find other solutions to handle or minimize the enormous crowds.

In hopes of lowering our attendance to a more manageable level, we increased the general admission price to two dollars. This only caused a brief slow up and by 2001 the attendance was back up to what it was when only charging a dollar. Between 2001 and 2003, The Byrd was patronized even more than when the theatre had

Disney exclusively in 1989.

Another way to increase profits was to increase theatre rentals which were not subject to admissions tax levied on all movie theaters in the City of Richmond. So most film festivals, music concerts, plays, and the like were all posted in the ledgers as theatre rentals. This would save about seven percent to the box office bottom line. If the rentals came from a non-profit organization, like the French Film Festival, the admissions tax would be forgiven outright.

Still another source of income outside of movie exhibitions came from paid screen ad placements. The Byrd may have been the first movie theatre in the country to advertise non-movie ads on the screen before movie presentations.

These still ads were projected by the Brenograph projectors that were original to the theatre in 1928 and used extensively for theatre organ accompaniment sing-a-longs. Everyone was accustomed to the relentless showing of upcoming movie attractions, which we all dislike with a passion. There is nothing worse than rushing to attend a movie showing only to sit through a half hour of coming attractions. That wouldn't have helped the Byrd anyway; the Byrd was the last stop for movies shown before being released on video.

Screen ads were always shown on the silver screen and always before the feature advertised show times. This gave the audience something to entertain them before the show began—talk about a captive audience. Screen advertisements could bring in as much as $2000 a month in additional income and allowed more time for patrons to visit the concession counter.

At show time, the organist rising from the bowels of the theatre would notify patrons the movie was about to begin.

The Mighty Wurlitzer

SPECIAL ENGAGEMENT
AN EXTRAORDINARY
EVENT

WINGS

BYRD SINCE 1928

ADMIT ONE · ANY REGULAR

ADMIT ONE · ANY REGULAR

ADMIT ONE · ANY REGULAR

ADMIT ONE

VIP PASS · ANY REGULAR OR SP· BYR

Fanfare,

For 67 years, the Byrd Thea... resplendent. Even now, worn... elegance lacking at the multi-plexes... digital audio tape; the Byrd is Mozart...

The theater's uniqueness is not... Often the best part of the evening is... organ rises from below floor level and L... side, house organist, belts out the Wur... wind's big-wind sounds — and it's almost... Eddie Weaver all over again — and it's a little... campy, like the flapper-girl costumes worn by... the concessionaires — but then the camp is... half the fun.

The other half is listening to a live... performance with an instrument few today... ever get to hear. Now, Richmonders who... enjoy listening to the Wurlitzer when they go out can enjoy it when they stay... The Virginia Theater Organ Society and the Byrd have conspired to release... Byrd Sings," a compact disc of recordings made with the Wurlitzer... Ron Rhode plays the instrument for the recording: Chuck Rhode... vocals. The scores range from the Cavalleria Rusticana intermezzo to "I'm... Over a Four-Leaf Clover." The CD is available at local music stores, ... itself, of course, remains on Cary Stree... fortune, it will stay open for a long ...

THE PICTURE
THE PICTURE

Richmond's Historic
Byrd Theatre

CHAPTER TWENTY-TWO
Carytown Promotions

The Byrd Theatre's stage made the facility a perfect venue for music. The acoustics were good, the sight lines were good and in the mid-1990s Richmond needed a good medium size music hall. A problem with renting the Byrd out to promoters was that they always wanted to book shows on Friday or Saturday nights. Preempting a movie for a live show would yield more profit, but it would also cause a breach in consistency of format. As I would say over and over again, consistency in any business is the golden rule.

Not long after the theatre retired "Art Afternoons at the Byrd," several promoters came by the Theatre one day to talk music. Laurence Jones and Wilbur Smith of Carytown Promotions represented a handful of investors and friends who wanted to promote jazz concerts on Sunday afternoons. What a perfect solution to a normally slow time! The only problem was that the theatre didn't have any dressing rooms to accommodate the musicians but what the Byrd offered to make up for it was a medium size auditorium that filled a void in the Richmond market.

The huge Mosque seated 3,500 patrons and the Carpenter Center for the Performing Arts around 2,100 patrons. Other music venues were much smaller lounges and bars and could accommodate only a few hundred patrons for smaller acts. So, the Byrd at 1,300 seats was a perfect venue for medium size concerts.

Unfortunately, the music promotions business is high risk.

There are times in the year that don't yield well for indoor concerts, there are risks from bad weather, competitive risks, and for some entertainers (i.e. Jerry Lee Lewis) there is the risk that the entertainment may not show up. Regardless, a promoter still must pay the venue rent and for all of the advertising and promotions that go along with the entertainment.

For the Byrd, the rent was imperative. Unlike other "not for profit" venues that could afford to go dark, the Byrd needed a continuous steady flow of business to fill her seats. So Jones, Smith, and their company, Carytown Promotions, brought in ten jazz artists over the course of a three month period.

Artists like The Rippingtons, Hiroshima, David Sanborn, Patti Labelle and Chick Corea graced the stage of the Byrd Theatre, bringing some incredible jazz sounds to Richmond.

One of my favorites, Chick Corea, was a Yamaha representative and performed on one of the only two Yamaha Concert Grand Pianos available in the country. The CFX full concert grand piano was so large and heavy, there were great concerns over whether or not the piano would fit on the stage and whether or not the stage floor would support such a heavy instrument. But everything about the Byrd was "beefed up" and there was really no cause for concern. To see and hear such great artists in the Byrd was a treat.

The Byrd had now been open and running under my direction for more than two years. Not that I ever had any feelings of financial security, the Byrd was paying the bills on a timely basis. I was not kiting quite so many checks and was submitting monthly rent payments towards the beginning of the month versus towards the end of the month. All of the employees were getting paid on time and all of the payroll taxes were being submitted on time.

Personally, I was making $200 a week, which was $100 less than I was making when working with Cable and the Tobacco Company Restaurant. I couldn't afford an apartment of my own, so I spent a lot of those sleepless hours on anyone's sofa that was a comfortable seven feet long and inviting. Of course I was getting tired of this, but I didn't want to spend anything on an apartment—anything that would take me away from reaching my dream of sailing around the world. I really needed to save every penny, nickel, and dime so I could eventually buy a boat of my own.

CHAPTER TWENTY-THREE
The Red Badge of Courage

In 1992, Randy Strawderman introduced to me his idea of a musical adaptation of Stephen Crane's *The Red Badge of Courage*. This would be a phenomenal production and a wonderful opportunity to present Crane's literary masterpiece on stage.

The Red Badge of Courage was required reading for all of us growing up, probably because its story line is so universal for youth coming of age, regardless of the time or place in history. Although *The Red Badge of Courage* takes place in the Civil War, it could have taken place in any war, anywhere, past, present, or future.

Along with the presentation, Strawderman and I introduced a new financial concept that would allow The Colonel Read Foundation for Courage in the Arts to workshop new theatrical productions using charitable funding, and then move the same, but finished theatrical productions to a profit seeking venture using much of the same capital.

This concept was used to fund *The Red Badge of Courage*. In a nutshell, an individual could take the tax advantages of contribution and at the same time be granted a percentage of stock in another company as an investment. From the beginning, *The Red Badge of Courage* was developed to open and show on Broadway in New

York City.

Initially, Strawderman's theatrical concept started with a single song written and composed by Robbin Thompson and Carlos Chafin titled "Sing a Song of Victory." Although originally the song was performed a capella by Thompson to many of the investors, when the theatrical production opened on a stage in front of a live audience years later, the song's composition would be fully orchestrated.

The means of funding a theatrical production is almost always difficult, especially one that is new and unproven. The initial budget to produce *Red Badge* was close to $600,000 while production costs of most Broadway shows at that time were running in the range of $8 to $10 million. To develop a possible Broadway production for just over a half million was considered quite reasonable. The actual production that opened at the Lenfest Center for the Arts at Washington and Lee University in Lexington, Virginia came to just under $400,000.

Most of the funding contributed to the Colonel Read Foundation for Courage in the Arts came from the Virginia Military Institute's Alumni Association in honor of Colonel Beverly Read. Among the VMI graduates contributing to the fund were some of Richmond, Virginia's, and this nation's strongest civic leaders and the captains of industry—such notables as Floyd Gottwald Jr., Bruce Gottwald, Billy Gottwald, Jim Migliarese, Teddy Gottwald, Elmon Gray, Bruce Gray and Stan Navas. Floyd Gottwald Jr, Elmon Gray, and Stan Navas all served in World War II.

Stan Navas was a great inspiration to Randy Strawderman and to me. Navas was the 1942 class president at Virginia Military Institute and lost his left arm while serving in WWII. He was president and CEO of Concrete Pipe and Products, and one of this nation's last great industrialists.

I will never forget the day when Strawderman first introduced *The Red Badge of Courage* to Navas. Strawderman went into Navas' office with just a boombox and a recording of Robbin Thompson's a capella version of "Sing a Song of Victory." Within an hour, Strawderman emerged with a huge check in his hand.

If only Navas' health had remained with him a little longer, *The Red Badge of Courage* likely would have gone all the way to Broadway!

Funding *The Red Badge of Courage* opened new ways to pursue arts funding. Years later, this enabled us to find financial means to take the Byrd Theatre in a new direction. Most of the contributors for the Colonel Read Foundation were also contributors to the Byrd Theatre Foundation. Stan Navas wrote the first check.

By 1994, the Byrd was beginning to develop into her own and I started spending more and more time sailing the beautiful waters of the Rappahannock River and the Chesapeake Bay aboard my first yacht, *Courage*.

Ironically, *Courage* was not named after our theatrical presentation of *The Red Badge of Courage*, nor was it named after the non-profit entity from which the production was first presented, but after an English brewery of good taste founded by John Courage in 1787 in London, England.

I bought the boat used and as everyone will tell you, you should never change the name of a boat for it can bring the owner and the boat bad luck. I loved the name! This boat brought many things and taken me to many places, but never did the boat ever bring me bad luck.

Yacht *Courage* was a Cape Dory 33 built in 1984 in East Taunton, Massachusetts. A full keel, blue water boat, *Courage* was designed by Carl Alberg and was meant to be sailed offshore, and although I never left the safety of the Maryland and Virginia Intercoastal waterways of the Chesapeake Bay, if I had had the time, I would have sailed her across the Atlantic.

From the moment I went to Urbanna for that weekend sailing adventure years ago, I became infatuated with the sailing lifestyle. After all, with a last name like Nelson, not that I am claiming any relationship to my great, great, great … great grandfather Lord Horatio Nelson, one must still uphold that family name and its traditions

I read everything about sailing. I read the Horatio Hornblower novels by C.S. Forester. I read all of Patrick O'Brian's Aubrey-Maturin series of sea novellas. I read Chapman's *Piloting Seamanship and Small Boat Handling* three times. There wasn't anything I wouldn't read in regards to sailing, navigation, and seamanship.

I loved every bit of it and spent as much time on *Courage* and on the water as possible. *Courage* was my home. I couldn't afford both an apartment and a boat, so I chose the boat. And even though the Byrd was starting to turn a profit, it still wasn't doing well enough to afford a twenty-five percent down payment on a boat. So, being as fortunate and blessed as I am, my good friends Drs. David and Catherine White graciously bore the expense.

Eventually, the Byrd would not be my sole source of income. I was fortunate to have capitalized on the redevelopment of several historic properties throughout Richmond and the Carytown areas. By utilizing Federal and State tax credits designed to lure investments, I was eventually able to buy out the original investment parties and own the majority controlling interest in those properties. I also had the controlling management interest in other entertainment venues and restaurants throughout Virginia, Washington D.C. and Maryland.

For the development of Carytown and the surrounding neighborhoods, Richmond ACORN (Association of Community Organizations for Reform Now) awarded me Marguerite Cromley's prestigious "Golden Hammer Award" in 2003. To this day, I am still proud to have been honored with this award.

CHAPTER TWENTY-FOUR
Finding some Relief and a New Direction

In 1997, I ventured again north to see the Warrens. Instead of meeting the Warrens in Arlington as before, I met Mr. Warren and two of his children at a hotel they owned in Fredericksburg, Virginia. Mrs. Warren had since passed on.

My objectives were to alleviate the excruciating rent demanded by the Warrens, determine a means of replacing the old leaking roof and to discuss an alternative means of taking the Byrd Theatre into the future.

Having a non-profit organization as owner of the Byrd had always been on the table. Unfortunately, all of the non–profits approached didn't have the desire or the financial or organizational means to afford the theatre.

Most non-profit organizations originate from clubs, churches, and society groups, and are managed by enthusiasts from within those organizations; seldom are they professionally managed. Some of these smaller organizations approached were Richmond's Red Hat Society, The Richmond Jazz Society and some small theatrical groups in search of a home. These were all wonderful organizations, but they were also small.

The larger and more secure organizations in the Richmond

community that could afford the Byrd had no desire to undertake additional responsibilities, especially ones so large. Some of the organizations approached were the Richmond Symphony, Carytown Merchants Association, Virginia Commonwealth University, and The Virginia Theatre Organ Society. These were all good candidates, but owning and operating the Byrd would pose huge financial risks that no one wanted to take on.

By the end of the meeting with the Warrens, compromises and agreements were made. In lieu of rent, I would undertake the time and financial responsibility of forming a new 501(c)(3) nonprofit entity, The Byrd Theatre Foundation. I would continue to operate and maintain the theater until such a foundation could purchase it from the Estate of Irma and Samuel P. Warren.

The Warrens' commitment was that they would replace the existing roof with a new one. This would be the last time I would see Mr. Warren. Samuel and Irma Warren, at one time, were probably respectable, reasonable, fair, and good business-minded people. I was unfortunate to have not seen them in the prime of their lives. Even more unfortunate is that their children and heirs to their estate didn't seem to inherit the good business qualities and practices their parents must have possessed.

CHAPTER TWENTY-FIVE
The Track

Chris Liles opened the Track Restaurant in 1981. It was strategically located across from the Byrd Theatre— "strategically located" because I could escape the confines of the Byrd between shows, but could still keep a watchful eye on the goings-on at the theatre from across the street.

The Track wasn't a large restaurant by any means, seating only around sixty patrons. But in the 1990s, the Track was popular and often turned those seats over three or four times a night. Personalities, atmosphere, good cuisine and good service made the restaurant one of the most liked and successful in Richmond for a long time. Liles's specialties were seasonal favorites such as soft-shelled crabs in the summer, rockfish (striped bass) in the fall and shad roe in the winter. The two chefs I remember the most at the Track were Claude Broome and Chris Saladino.

I would meet some of the Byrd's most influential people at the Track. Creative people who would influence the many creative paths the Byrd would take over the course of my twenty-five year involvement. Some of the bartenders I met were Scottie McCracken, Andrew Ferguson, Lisa Callis and Pete Humes (an entire book could be written on Pete Humes and his contributions to the Byrd; this book will dedicate a mere chapter.)

Some of the patrons I met at the track were Sammy Marques, Ted Salins and Toby Gould. Sam is an actor and played in some of the Christmas shows; Salins is a filmmaker and a professor of film at John Tyler Community College and would often make it a point to tell me I knew nothing about films (I think Ted and Mike Jones hung out together) and then there was Toby Gould.

Toby Gould was a die-maker in Richmond. He worked in a factory five days a week and on Friday nights he would visit the Track and tell me stories of his younger days as a stagehand on New York City's Broadway and off-Broadway theater scene. As the story goes, Gould left New York and followed an actress to Richmond. She broke his heart and stranded him in Richmond never to return to New York City.

I kind of had the idea when first meeting Gould that a lot of his stories were just too big to be true and must have been made up, but as the years went by, Gould's stories proved to be even bigger than his representation and without exaggeration. He spoke a theater language only Randy Strawderman could pick up on.

He mentioned that his mother owned some theaters in New York's off-Broadway areas. Strawderman lived in New York City back in the 1970's and was familiar with all of Gould's New York theatrical landmark descriptions. Gould also mentioned being friends with Jason Robards and often would tell the gang, anyone present, the many stories of the shows he and Robards were in. Gould used to record on cassette tape many of the Byrd's Christmas show pre-production meetings at the Track; to listen to them now would be priceless.

On one of Strawderman and my first creativity enhancing trips to New York City, Gould mentioned a must visit to Sardi's Restaurant off Shubert Alley on Broadway. And then after Sardi's, a must visit to one of his old stomping grounds across 44th street called Johnny's.

Johnny's was a small restaurant on the second floor, similar to the

Track in appearance. Gould described it perfectly in every detail and when we mentioned Gould's name to the bartender, the bartender introduced us to the owner, Johnny. Johnny treated us with drinks, food and stories of when Gould and Robards would sit "right here" every night at his bar.

"Every night the two would tell stories of the many shows and stars," Johnny would say in a thick Italian accent, "You two are sitting in the very same seats Toby and Jason would sit in every night here at Johnny's."

Sure enough, on the back of the bar stools where we were seated were the names of Toby Gould and Jason Robards. Coincidentally, the bar stools at the Track Restaurant bear brass engravings the names of Duane Nelson, Randy Strawderman and Toby Gould.

CHAPTER TWENTY-SIX

Pete Humes, *Punchline* and Midnight Movies

The first time I met Pete Humes, he was bartending at the Track Restaurant. Pete Humes is funny. He has the type of personality and he presents himself in a way that if you don't listen closely, you're going to miss something, usually something very funny. He has a dry sense of humor and wit that will keep you on the edge of your conversational seat. He will throw in some sarcasm quite often, so when you meet him, and you *will* want to meet him, listen to everything he has to say.

When I met him, he was a student finishing up his major in Sculpture and Creative Writing at Virginia Commonwealth University's School of the Arts. He was working his way through school by bartending in a couple of restaurants and doing some work in some publications, one of them called the *Richmond Funny Paper*.

One night at the Track, Humes brought up the idea of publishing his own paper. He believed the now defunct *Richmond Funny Paper* could have become a publication sustained by local advertisers in the Richmond market. I listened. Humes made perfect sense.

Richmond, at that time, lacked a publication that attracted 18-to-35 year old readership. *Style Weekly* had been around for a while but appealed to a much older and more conservative market. Richmond didn't have a *City Paper, Village Voice* or an *Onion*-type publication which were all successful alternative publications in various parts of the country. What Richmond did have was Pete Humes.

The Byrd needed a way to target the younger audience.

In the late 1990s, the only advertising the Byrd was buying was with the *Richmond Times-Dispatch*. This was typically a 1x1-inch ad placed daily in the movie listings of the entertainment section. This advertising worked for the Byrd's discount mainstream films but didn't reach the younger audiences I wanted to promote for Midnight Movies.

At one time, Ray Bentley's Midnight Movies at the Ridge Cinema garnered great audiences, younger than 21 years of age, who couldn't patronize places serving alcohol, and for the most part didn't have anything better to do on a Friday or Saturday night. So, the idea of an alternative publication targeting those younger audiences captured my attention.

The plan was simple: take the now defunct *Richmond Funny Paper*, change the name, add some additional comic strips, and increase the advertising and distribution. Well, that idea lasted about a month; soon after its initial release, *Punchline* started publishing editorials, advertorials, commentaries and local and national news stories.

The collection of local comic strips grew to include big name syndicated cartoonists. The advertising campaigns grew from local "ma and pa" merchants to include much more lucrative national advertising campaigns. Bear in mind the local "ma and pa" businesses never went away, but grew and flourished and would remain a big part of the paper's heart, soul, and substance. In essence, *Punchline* became a *City Paper*, an alternative to anything else in Richmond, with a voice that reached Richmond's youth.

Punchline started as a monthly, went bi-weekly and then peaked at twenty thousand copies every week. It brought some of the most creative writers, artists and designers Richmond had ever seen together under one roof. So many people would give so much along the way. Most of them would work for grocery money. They didn't need a place to live—their homes were the offices of *Punchline*, and when they weren't working on their desk tops, they would try to catch a few winks under them.

So many wonderful creative works came out of *Punchline*, from the articles written and the caricatures drawn, to the ads created. *Punchline* also had a radio show. So, not only were the midnight movies advertised in the *Richmond Times-Dispatch* and *Punchline*, but also on the radio.

When the elephants were on our backs and we couldn't see beyond the fog, Liz Skrobiszewski stepped in. Liz was a big inspiration to all of us, and when we needed it the most, she brought in the hope and drive to keep things going. Besides *Punchline* and the Byrd, Liz helped create and launch WRIR, Richmond's first independent low-power FM radio station!

Punchline began with an idea from Pete Humes. And as the same type of idea restarted the Byrd Theatre in 1984, it took the same type of dedication, work ethic, dreams, and desires to achieve. In the end, all of us found that there was a cost—a cost that shouldn't have to be paid.. The Byrd Theatre and *Punchline* were carried on the backs of hard working folks for many years, putting in endless hours without sleep, and always meeting those dreaded deadlines. Both the Byrd and *Punchline* were successful, but seldom were either financially profitable.

Eventually, you have to look at life as a whole. And when you can take the time to take a breath, you will find there is so much to live for. Sometimes you have to trade in the things that drive you now for things that you want in the future.

For Pete Humes and Liz Skrobiszewski, it was a family; for me, it was things like the culinary arts, sailing and adventure. Humes and Skrobiszewski traded in their marriage with *Punchline* for a marriage to each other.

Punchline was such a big and important part of our lives!

Thanks to *Punchline*, midnight movies in Richmond were big again, but this time at the Byrd Theatre. On average, midnight movies drew over a thousand patrons a show on Friday and Saturday nights. The patrons were there to have a good time, to get out of the house, maybe just to get away from their parents and if they felt like it, they could even watch a movie.

The Byrd never showed *The Rocky Horror Picture Show* (too big of a mess.) But it did show the *Goonies* probably more times than anyone would like to remember. And, the Byrd would always bring in cult films like *The Big Lebowski, Blade Runner, A Clockwork Orange, Fight Club, Pulp Fiction* and *Plan 9 from Outer Space*.

Every so often the Ululating Mummies would make an appearance and provide the music to what would normally be a silent film. And always a big favorite was playing *The Wizard of Oz*, but with Pink Floyd's album, *The Dark Side of the Moon* as the soundtrack. Midnight movies at the Byrd were definitely fun!

THE BYRD THEATRE

RAY LIOTTA   ROBERT DE NIRO   JOE PESCI

SATURDAY NIGHT MIDNIGHT MOVIES

ADMISSION IS ONLY $3

SATURDAY JAN. 5

GoodFellas

SATURDAY JAN. 12
THE GOONIES

SATURDAY JAN. 19
THE PRINCESS BRIDE

SATURDAY JAN. 26
THE NEVERENDING STORY

Midnight Movies at the Byrd

Showing this Saturday, February 24th
Only 7

Fritz Lang's METROPOLIS

with live performance by the Ululating Mummies

Showing Saturday, March 3rd
Only 3
THE EXORCIST

Showing Saturday, March 10th
The Stewardesses
THE SCREEN COMES ALIVE IN...
STEREOVISION 3D
Only 5

THE UNPUBLISHABLE NOVEL IS NOW AMERICA'S MOST CONTROVERSIAL FILM!

THE BYRD THEATRE

Sponsored by TECHEAD and Nelson Communications

2908 West Cary Street (in Carytown)
353-9911
Free parking behind the theatre

CHAPTER TWENTY-SEVEN
Forming the Foundation

The Byrd Theatre Foundation was actually the second 501(c) (3) organization I formed; the first being The Colonel Read Foundation for Courage in the Arts formed back in 1992 with Randy Strawderman. Organizing The Byrd Theatre Foundation was much more difficult.

Section 501(c)(3) of the Internal Revenue Code states, "A 501(c) (3) organization is a corporation, trust, unincorporated association, or other type of organization that is exempt from federal income tax under section 501(c)(3)of title 26 of the United States Code."

To obtain this designation, an organization must undergo a long and complicated process, often involving many applications. Although an organization can raise funds while an application is still pending, in order to form a board of directors, the Byrd Theatre Foundation had to be approved by the Internal Revenue Service to be tax exempt under the terms of section 501(c)(3) of the Internal Revenue Code.

The Colonel Read Foundation for Courage in the Arts types of organizations often were being approved by the IRS with minimal documentation. Their design was to preserve some portion of a dying art. Movies may be an art form, but never have they been on an endangered species list. Recognizing preservation of the building alone probably would have been an easy application, but to preserve "education" aspects of the foundation, such as preserving and presenting theatre organ, silent film accompaniment and movie exhibition were something for which the IRS seldom had received application.

The process for applying for exempt status began in 1998 and it wasn't until the spring of 2002 that the Byrd Theatre Foundation finally received its tax exempt designation. Hirschler Fleischer was the law firm that undertook the tedious task of continuous application. This cost me just over $17,000 for their efforts, which in essence became the foundation's first contributions. Upon receiving exempt status, the next step was to appoint a board of directors, begin a fundraising campaign, and begin negotiations towards purchasing the Theatre.

Forming a board of directors was difficult. Because of potential liability issues, only a handful of the initial potential board members asked would accept a position as directors. Although this selection process had begun before the tax exempt designation was granted, it wasn't until Tony Pelling stepped up to help that things started moving forward.

In the spring of 2002, I stepped down as the President of the Byrd Theatre Foundation in favor of Tony Pelling. Pelling and I agreed that in order to minimize the appearance of a conflict of interest between me and the Foundation, I couldn't even be at arm's length to the Foundation. Also, tension was building between the owners of the property and me largely because the leaking roof was never replaced.

These negotiations needed to happen on a somewhat peaceful playing field and this wouldn't happen as long as the owners and the operator were in the same room. Even so, the negotiations did not proceed smoothly. It took five years of effort, one and a half years longer than expected, to purchase the building.

Stepping down as president of the Foundation was difficult because it meant I couldn't be a part of a dream I envisioned and had been working to accomplish for many years. I described this as being like Moses, the leader to the Promised Land, but not being allowed to lead once in the Promised Land. But through it all, the Foundation and I knew that for the Byrd Theatre to succeed in the future, it must be owned and operated by the Foundation, and it is!

By the year 2002, everything was going well, and for the first time I felt it might be possible to pursue my lifelong dream of sailing around the world. But to accomplish this by 2005, a lot of things had to happen.

I was without a boat and living in a house on Newport Avenue in the Ginter Park/Belmont area of Richmond's Northside. I liked this house and bought it with the idea of getting married and raising children. Not that this idea doesn't still intrigue me, but in 2002, the timing just wasn't right.

It would be tough to sail around the world with a wife and a couple of bambinos on a boat, regardless of the size of the boat. Besides, sailing the oceans and seas of the world is mysterious and a wonderful adventure, but it can also be dangerous.

So, the first things to go were all of the properties and toys that wouldn't fit on the boat. I had a girlfriend I liked very much, but taking her away from Richmond, her career, her family, and friends was not on the table. Sailing was something I wanted to do, but I would need to do it alone.

I was fortunate to have had a great girlfriend in Sharlee Crone, I am even more fortunate to still have her as a good friend. Sharlee is a Virginia Tech graduate, so every September we text or call each other to compare notes on the new season and the Hokies football team.

Since I didn't have a boat and needed one to go sailing, I started to search for one that was large enough to be comfortable, but not so large it couldn't be handled by one person. My search started in a *Soundings* publication; a publication that listed thousands of new and used boats for sale all over the world.

The search would also take Sharlee and me to Annapolis, MD and a half a dozen small cities and towns along the East Coast where we would spend many weekends crawling and rummaging through boats on creeks, rivers, lakes and in back yards. The enjoyable part of searching was seeing all of the beautiful boats; the difficulty would be in choosing the right one.

The boat I eventually settled on was a Ta Shing Panda 38 named *Skybird*. This was one of only twenty-four Panda 38's built in the world—she was beautifully appointed in teak and mahogany, and fitted with brass, bronze and stainless steel fixtures.

I did keep one thing from the old boat to be transferred to the new one; a book written by Joshua Slokum titled, *Sailing Alone Around the World*. It was written in 1900 by Slokum upon the completion of his record breaking accomplishment—he was the first man to sail single-handedly around the world. This is a great book, but the similarities with Slokum's sailing adventures and mine end with the single-handed part.

Slokum's boat, *Spray*, was a wooden sailboat with no auxiliary power, no electricity, only oil lanterns lighting her berths, and only a sextant for navigation. *Skybird*, on the other hand, has an auxiliary diesel engine, a diesel generator for electricity, a hot and cold pressurized water system, and navigation equipment using a Global Positioning System, which is a good thing, because the only thing I can find with a sextant is a pounding headache and a dark spot in my eyes from staring into the sun.

By the fall of 2005, I was ready; the foundation was ready; everyone in Richmond was ready. I figured I could sail as far south as Charleston, SC by New Years, rent a car, drive back to Richmond and turn the Byrd Theatre over to the foundation. This way, the foundation could own and start operating the Byrd Theatre by January 1, 2006.

If things had happened on that schedule, the foundation would have taken over the theatre in good standings and with good momentum. Unfortunately, things didn't happen on that schedule and it would take the foundation an excruciating extra year and a half of negotiations to eventually purchase the Byrd.

CHAPTER TWENTY-EIGHT
Shall No Good Deed Go Unpunished

The foundation was formed in 2002, at which time I introduced the Byrd Theatre Foundation to the Warrens' heirs. The sole purpose of this meeting was to begin negotiations for the Foundation's acquisition of the Byrd Theatre.

The heirs seemed to have difficulty determining an offering price for the Byrd, so I spent another $4,000 to have the property appraised at $700,000. The purpose of this appraisal was to encourage the heirs to do what most do in a situation such as this and donate the property to the Foundation.

Philanthropy did not prevail and it took them five years (one and a half years longer than expected) to negotiate a selling price of more than $1,200,000, $500,000 above the appraised value of the property. And then, the heirs turned around and sued Nelson Communications Company, the theatre's operating company, for the five years back rent not paid during the time spent negotiating the Foundation's acquisition of the theatre.

Unfortunately, I was mostly away for those one and a half unexpected years and couldn't oversee the management of the theatre's operations. The Byrd lost over $100,000 and many of the foundation's board members resigned over the frustration of the never-ending delays.

I had to sell most of the antique furniture in the theatre to cover the losses and the Foundation had to recruit new board members. Many Richmonders worked good deeds for many years to save the Byrd Theatre, only to have it nearly taken away in the end.

Why? I don't know. Maybe because no good deed should go unpunished? Lawsuits can be complicated and it's important to have the best legal representation when handling such matters. I was fortunate to have a brilliant attorney in Sean Tluchak and the lawsuit was settled with no monies being exchanged.

CHAPTER TWENTY-NINE
We Did It Well

Upon the passing of Miles Rudisill and my writing of the letter to the Whitten family at the beginning of this book, I felt there was an interest and a need to write about the Byrd Theatre.

After all, I devoted close to a quarter of a century of my life to the survival of the Byrd. I wrote the original manuscript of this book in third person. Primarily because I wanted to use the words "I" and "my" as little as possible, and I wanted to act more as a narrator in a book that tells the story of the Byrd Theatre and about all of those individuals without whose help, the Byrd Theatre may not have survived.

To say the theatre "would not" have survived would show a bit of arrogance on my part. It's difficult to say if our efforts during those trying years were the only path the Byrd Theatre could have taken to succeed, so let's simply say the Byrd Theatre was extremely blessed to survive some difficult times and now, more than ten years after the foundation purchased the theatre; she is still open, still being restored, and still entertaining Richmonders.

I have been saving the most important thanks and praise for last. To all of the house managers and employees of the Byrd Theatre I thank you! If it wasn't for your shining faces, pretty smiles and charming ways, I know for certain that the Byrd Theatre would not have survived and thrived.

Being in the front of the house, welcoming all of the patrons can sometimes feel like being on the front line of a battlefield. You would think that by charging only a dollar or two that everyone entering the beautiful Byrd Theatre would be happy. You would think.

I can't remember my own name half the time, so this will only be a few who worked at the Byrd Theatre from 1984-2007. Starting in 1984: David Sadler, Mary Burruss, Brandon Fox, Adrien Arnold, Kim Wood, Alan George, Tina Boling, Lara Koplin, Jenna Anderson, Cindy Howell, Courtney Bowles, Karen Labrador, Scott Hudgins, Cameron Adams, Michael Pacaud, Brandon Fox, Reeves Smith, Sara Brown, Claire Ashby, Zoe Houchens, Liz Sparks, Elisa Nader, LeeAnne(Audrey)Ball, Amanda Camp, Amy Bucklen, Kathy Crowder, Aaron Blum, Peter Hopewell, Amy Ross, Paul Thompson, Ronnie Bradberry, James Jordan, Carl Hawk, Scott Eaton, Ballard Preston, Bill Anderson, Ross Southward, Danny Willis, Eddie Thornhill, Paul Cruser, Jeff Reid, Paul Bethel, Claire Ashby, Gary Romberg, Lynn Harrell, Jeanette Posner, Lisa Miller, Richard Morton, Rebecca Plate, Gary Talbott, Adalia Shchurowsky, Rob Miller, Johnny Cecka, Brian Harvey, Ben Forgey, Barry Robbins, and last but not least, Todd Schall-Vess. All of you did a great job!

I would like to give a special thanks to Todd Schall-Vess. He had the dubious honor of moving the operations of Nelson Communications Company trading as the Byrd Theatre to the non-profit operation of the Byrd Theatre Foundation. He went from working for one person, me, to working for an entire board of directors. I could not have done it, but he did, and he did it in fine fashion.

When writing about the Byrd, it's always easy to end on a good note, especially when that note is played by Bob Gulledge. Bob Gulledge has been the Byrd Theatre's organist for close to twenty-five years. He has absolutely been one of the Byrd's most valuable ambassadors. He has a great sense of humor and wit that I seldom have had the privilege to see in anyone.

Also, after knowing Bob for many years and having the pleasure of working with him, I know that when he says he is going to get something done, you can believe he will get it done. You can always count on Bob.

Once, during a Fourth of July weekend, Bob, Gary Cowardin, Bill Enos, and I were congregating in the lobby before the 7:15 p.m. show. We did this quite often. We talked about the show "biz" or the movie showing that night, usually something to do with the Byrd. This evening, the topic of our conversation was "standing ovations." Seldom would an organist ever receive a standing ovation—maybe for a live presentation, but never for a movie or pre-movie presentation.

That night, Bob guaranteed a standing ovation.

He whispered something in Bill's ear. Bill went upstairs to the projection booth, Bob headed towards the basement to the theatre organ and Gary and I just scratched our heads in wonder.

Wow, what a surprise!

We never considered Bob would finish his pre-movie organ spot playing the National Anthem. Why would we? I've heard the National Anthem played at sporting events and presidential ceremonies, but never before a movie.

Bob came through as usual. Everyone was standing—everyone! I've never been in a more patriotic movie theatre than the Byrd!

All of us involved at the Byrd Theatre always did our best and often for little money ... or no money at all. The joy and satisfaction of preserving the Byrd Theatre and entertaining so many Richmonders was all the compensation we sought. In essence, our payment came by means of the applause. The real saviors of the Byrd Theatre were not necessarily those individuals donating their time and efforts, but the many patrons who visited the Byrd and were entertained—the citizens of Richmond, Virginia.

I always dreamed for the adventure, to see what was on the other side, do something different and to do something that would make a difference in someone's life. I feel as if I did make a difference for the good in Richmond.

And to leave Richmond when I did, where most of my friends lived, where many of my successes were, and where I lived for twenty-five years, was tough. But, unlike George Bailey in *It's a Wonderful Life*, I did see some of the world. Upon leaving the Byrd and Richmond in the spring of 2007, I sailed as far north as Halifax, Nova Scotia, as far east as Ponta Delgada, Azores and as far South as Colon, Panama.

As far as golf is concerned, one day I would like to play at least one more round with all of my friends who live in and around the Richmond and Charlottesville areas or wherever there are trees and sand. Oh, how I miss playing out of the woods and into all of the courses' sand traps. If only I could remember the course and the lake where I last stored my clubs! As far as the adventure in sailing is concerned; I am thinking more and more about the west coasts of the Americas, the South Pacific and the Indian Ocean. But, in my mind is probably where those adventures will stay.

In the years away from Richmond, I have also spent a lot of time exploring new ideas and developing new businesses. But, I will always look back on my years at the Byrd Theatre with fond memories. We did what many said couldn't be done and we did it well.

There's no business like show business!

MEMORABILIA
From My Collection

The Byrd Theatre

The BYRDETTES

Academy Award Winner

SPECIAL ENGAGEMENT
AN EXTRAORDINARY
EVENT

'WINGS

1927

Considered one of the best war [films ever]
made. This epic of World War [I stars Clara]
Bow, Charles "Buddy" Rogers[, Richard Ar-]
len, and Gary Cooper. It was [the last of the]
great silent films, and will [be accompanied]
by Lin Lunde at the consol[e of the famous]
Byrd Theatre pipe organ, [playing the origi-]
nal musical score. For thi[s unusual presen-]
tation, there will be no a[dvance in prices.]

Mon–Wed
Eight PM only

Aug. 13–15

SPECIAL ENGAGEMENT
AN EXTRAORDINARY
EVENT

WINGS

1927

Considered one of the best war films ever
made. This epic of World War I stars Clara
Bow, Charles "Buddy" Rogers, Richard Ar-
len, and Gary Cooper. It was the last of the
great silent films, and will be accompanied
by Lin Lunde at the console of the famous
Byrd Theatre pipe organ, playing the original musical score. For this unusual presentation, there will be no advance in prices.

FRIDAY

NOVEMBER 1

The Byrd Theatre
Christmas Celebration
Friday, Dec. 5 — Sunday, Dec. 7
PRESENTING
Lin Lunde
AT THE MIGHTY WURLITZER

David Newman
AT THE WURLITZER GRAND

Chuck Rhode
LYRIC TENOR

David Hirschi
MASTER JUGGLER

The Byrdettes
RICHMOND'S FAVORITE HIGH-KICKING DANCERS

ON THE SCREEN
"Miracle on 34th Street"
and a classic cartoon

Friday - Sunday at 8:00
Special Sunday Matinee at 3:00

THE BYRD THEATRE
2908 West Cary Street, Richmond, Virginia 23221

PROGRAM

The
BYRD
"Richmond's Theatre
Beautiful"

5 Days Commencing
Sat., December 19

Next Attraction
STARTING
Christmas Day
SETH PARKER in
"Way Back
Home"
A Radio Picture

THE BYRDETTES

WOULD YOU LIKE TO BE A BYRDETTE?

If you think you have the necessary re-
quirements to be a line dancer on the
stage of The Byrd Theatre, this is to
advise you that auditions will be held
on Saturday and Su~   February 8 and
9, at 2:00 p.m.   Theatre,
2908 West Cary
in mind that ar
sarily guarante
your   tap sh
Paid   perfor
and Saturd
Easter w
please c

Buster Keaton's Funniest
"THE CAMERAMAN"

Accompanied by
LIN LUNDE
at the "Mighty Wurlitzer"

Jan. 23 & 24 8 p.m.

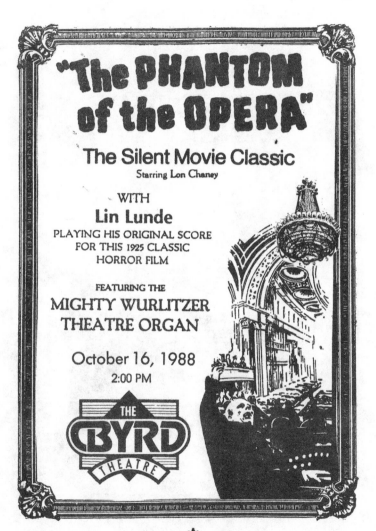

"The PHANTOM of the OPERA"

The Silent Movie Classic
Starring Lon Chaney

WITH

Lin Lunde

PLAYING HIS ORIGINAL SCORE
FOR THIS 1925 CLASSIC
HORROR FILM

FEATURING THE
MIGHTY WURLITZER
THEATRE ORGAN

October 16, 1988
2:00 PM

THE
BYRD
THEATRE

James River Festival of the Moving Image & Nelson Communications

Buster Keaton in

The General

Saturday April 12 1997 Midnight $5.00

Live Accompaniment by the Ululating Mummies

A Buster Keaton Laugh Riot!
"THE GENERAL"

A Classic of the Silent Screen

ENCOUNTERS OF THE FUNNIEST KIND!

THE GENERAL (1927) Buster Keaton stars in this 1927 film in which the silent comedy reached its zenith. This is the favorite silent comedy shown today. The General does not refer to Keaton, but rather to his locomotive which played a vital role in our Civil War. The story takes place in the South and is based on an incident that actually happened in 1862. Keaton plays the role of Johnnie Gray and Marion Mack is Annabelle Lee, his helpless leading lady. Lin Lunde will accompany this film on the famous Byrd Theatre Wurlitzer, providing all the effects that an old-time locomotive requires.

FRIDAY
OCTOBER 18

A Charlie Chaplin Festival

Starring the King of Comedy

"MODERN TIMES"

"THE KID"

"One A.M."
"The Pawnshop"
"The Floorwalker"
"The Rink"

February 4 - 10

We are happy to include Lyn Lunde on the Wurlitzer as part of The Byrd's exciting weekend entertainment. Lyn, who has been associated with The Byrd for nearly ten years, has made concert performances throughout the east coast and has completed the concert recording: *The Mosque Wurlitzer.* Well known in Richmond, Lyn has also appeared extensively at The Mosque and at numerous classical organ recitals. Lyn will perform at The Byrd Friday and Saturday evenings before the final show and on Sunday before the evening's first performance.

Rudolph Valentino

IN

"THE EAGLE"

Accompanied by Lin Lunde at the Mighty Wurlitzer

February 18-21

ACKNOWLEDGMENTS

I would like to thank David Barnett, Pete Humes, and Cathy Plageman for their wonderful editorial support in writing this first book. I would like to thank Adrien Arnold for helping me remember just a handful of the many employees that worked at and were a big part of making the Byrd Theatre so special. Also, Wendy Daniel for making the book look great. And especially Joni Albrecht and Little Star Communications for making this book possible.

ABOUT THE AUTHOR

Duane Kennedy Nelson studied engineering at Virginia Poly-technic Institute and State University. He studied business admin-istration, advertising, and marketing at Virginia Commonwealth University. He studied sailing and seamanship in the North Atlantic. He is learning how to make Pastyempanadas and how to write. He lives aboard his yacht Skybird somewhere between the Virginia Chesapeake Bay and the Lesser Antilles of the Caribbean Sea.